Unveiling Treasure Heists
Chronicles Of Riches

Unveiling Treasure Heists Chronicles Of Riches

Rafeal Mechlore

UNIEK ENTERPRISES

CONTENTS

INDEX

Introduction

1. Introduction to the allure of treasure heists
2. Setting the stage for the book's exploration

Introduction

The world has forever been enamored by accounts of greatness, richness, and abundance past creative mind. All through the records of mankind's set of experiences, the quest for wealth has molded human advancements, lighted conflicts, and filled the fantasies of innumerable people. These fantasies of fortune have frequently prompted trying accomplishments and, periodically, to more obscure deeds. In the pages of history, there are stories of amazing fortunes amassed over hundreds of years, drawing the consideration of globe-trotters, archeologists, and, in some cases, clever hoodlums.

The quest for riches and the appeal of fortune have been persevering through topics in human life. A mission rises above limits of time, geology, and culture. From the old pharaohs of Egypt to the extravagant heads of Rome, from the conquerors of the New World to the cutting edge big shots of Money Road, riches and the fortunes it presents have consistently held an exceptional spot in the human mind.

The interest with treasure isn't bound to the domain of legend or fiction. Countless genuine fortunes exist, each with its own set of experiences and persona. These fortunes come in different structures, from sparkling diamonds to many-sided workmanship pieces, from antiquated compositions to valuable metals. The narratives behind these fortunes are all around as different as the actual fortunes, and they range from stories of success and provincial double-dealing to archeological revelations that have changed how we might interpret history.

Nonetheless, one part of the fortune account that reliably catches the aggregate creative mind is the idea of fortune heists. These trying capers, frequently including crafty and brassy lawbreakers, stand as a demonstration of the lengths individuals will go to in quest for riches. The daringness of fortune heists frequently brings about sensational accounts that rival the best works of fiction, yet they remain genuine and, much of the time, inexplicable problems that keep on confounding specialists and dazzle the general population.

Uncovering Fortune Heists: Narratives of Wealth dives into this absolutely exhilarating and baffling universe of fortune heists. It reveals the tales of probably the most nervy robberies ever, and the people who, in light of multiple factors, gambled with everything for an opportunity at unbelievable riches. While these heists have caught the public's creative mind, they have additionally uncovered the weaknesses in our reality's mother lodes and the complexities of defending what society considers socially and generally huge.

From the beginning of time, treasure heists have been firmly connected to the more extensive development of craftsmanship, culture, and governmental issues. Whether persuaded by the craving for privately invested money, public pride, or political plans, these burglaries have had sweeping outcomes. The taken fortunes themselves frequently change hands on various occasions, and they can become pawns in world-wide fights for control, transforming taken workmanship into political prisoners and stole verifiable ancient rarities into objects of question.

It's critical to comprehend that fortune heists are not just about the deficiency of important items; they address a break in the common agreement that keeps developments intact. At the point when fortune is taken, it denies society of a common legacy, slicing connections to the past and subverting the underpinnings of our social character. These heists bring up fundamental issues about how we esteem and safeguard our common history and the lengths we will go to guarantee these fortunes are protected for people in the future.

Treasure heists, while frequently inspired by covetousness, can likewise be driven by an inborn human interest with the obscure and the impossible. The mystery and persona encompassing secret fortunes have the influence to light the creative mind, similar as the legendary stories of stowed away urban areas of gold or lost privateer accumulates. The general thought of a secret store of wealth requests to the globe-trotter in each one of us, mixing a yearning for the excitement of disclosure, regardless of whether that revelation comes through unlawful means.

This interest with stowed away fortunes has led to a subculture of fortune trackers who, albeit not really lawbreakers, are still up in the air to uncover these unbelievable wealth. From the profundities of the sea to far off mountains and thick woodlands, they set out on journeys driven by legends, bits of gossip, and authentic records, wanting to find the fortunes that have long evaded others. Their accounts frequently obscure the line between genuine investigation and crime, as the line between treasure tracker and fortune hoodlum is many times a slim one.

In Uncovering Fortune Heists, we investigate this spellbinding existence where truth and fiction entwine. We inspect the inspirations, the techniques, and the outcomes of these trying robberies and the endeavors to recuperate taken treasures. In doing as such, we shed light on the more obscure parts of our set of experiences and the persevering through effect of these burglaries on the social orders they influence.

This investigation drives us to the absolute most renowned and getting through treasure heists ever. From the shameless robbery of the Mona Lisa in 1911 to the vanishing of the Russian Golden Room during The Second Great War, these heists are something other than wrongdoings; they are sections in a bigger story of human desire, interest, and fixation. As we dive into these accounts, we find that the inspirations driving fortune heists are just about as differed as the actual fortunes.

A few cheats are driven by unadulterated eagerness, looking to hoard fortunes by selling taken treasures on the underground market. Others are inspired by patriotism, expecting to localize social antiques that they accept were illegitimately taken by unfamiliar powers. There are the people who participate in heists as a type of dissent against the establishments that they see as oppressors or as a method for pointing out a specific reason. While their thought processes might contrast, the daringness and shrewd expected to execute such wrongdoings tie them together in a trap of interest and risk.

The results of fortune heists reach out past the prompt burglary and the possible monetary benefits. They frequently bring about an overall manhunt, catch the creative mind of the media and people in general, and lead to broad examinations by policing and associations entrusted with shielding social legacy. The recuperation of taken treasures, when it happens, can be an account of equity winning, yet the lacking parts frequently leave a void that resounds all through the universe of craftsmanship and relics.

Revealing Fortune Heists likewise wanders into the mind boggling universe of workmanship fraud and the job it plays in both powering and forestalling treasure heists. The charm of taken loves frequently propels counterfeiters to make imitations that are persuading to the point that they can without much of a stretch bamboozle gatherers, galleries, and policing. These frauds further confound the undertaking of recuperating taken craftsmanship, as examiners should filter through layers of double dealing to uncover reality.

The quest for taken treasures isn't restricted to the universe of policing exhibition halls; it likewise includes a tremendous organization of people and associations focused on protecting social legacy. This people group incorporates archeologists, workmanship students of history, specialists, and activists who commit their lives to finding taken loves and pushing for their re-visitation of their legitimate spots. Their endeavors are vigorous, and they frequently work in the shadows, teaming up across worldwide lines to uncover reality and look for equity.

The universe of fortune heists isn't restricted to any one period or geological area. It traverses the globe, addressing essentially every development and period in mankind's set of experiences. The robbery of fortunes from the burial chambers of old pharaohs in Egypt, the plundering of extremely valuable antiquities during the disorder of war, and the daring burglaries of present day craftsmanship displays are all essential for this complex story.

Disclosing Fortune Heists takes you on an excursion through time and across mainlands, winding around together the strings of these accounts to introduce an exhaustive perspective on the enamoring universe of taken treasures and the people who try to recuperate them. We investigate the brassy burglaries and tricky plots that definitely stand out, from the shocking heist at the Isabella Stewart Gardner Historical center to the vanishing of the Nizam's gems in India.

As we dig into these accounts, we come to comprehend that fortune heists are not segregated occasions but rather are profoundly associated with the more extensive human experience. They mirror the intricacies of our set of experiences, our continuous journey for information, and our persevering through interest with abundance and the fortunes that address it.

While the dauntlessness of fortune heists might be stunning, the versatility of people and associations devoted to uncovering reality and it is similarly motivating to look for equity. Their energetic endeavors to recuperate taken fortunes and return them to their actual owners, be they countries, foundations, or people, help us to remember the influence of assurance and the significance of protecting our common history.

Disclosing Fortune Heists: Narratives of Wealth is an excursion into the profundities of human aspiration, covetousness, and fixation, where truth and fiction impact, and where the craving for abundance rises above limits of overall setting. It is a demonstration of the getting through charm of fortunes and the boldness of the individuals who look to have them, regardless of whether it implies violating the regulations that safeguard our social legacy. Through these pages, we reveal the secrets of fortune heists, analyze their effect on society, and eventually, shed light on the persevering through meaning of these accounts in the fabulous woven artwork of mankind's set of experiences.

1. **Introduction to the allure of treasure heists**

    Mankind's set of experiences is filled with stories of extravagance, riches, and fortune — stories that range the ages and areas of our reality, catching the creative mind of ages. The quest for wealth has molded realms, driven adventurers to the farthest corners of the globe, and energized dreams that have, on occasion, rose above the limits of the real world. Treasures, with their sparkling jewels, extremely valuable relics, and memorable importance, have held an extraordinary spot in human culture, starting our aggregate interest.

    The charm of fortune, whether as covered up privateer gold, old crowds, or lavish craftsmanship assortments, has an irrefutable hang on our mind. It takes advantage of our natural craving for riches, experience, and the excitement of revelation. However, underneath the outer layer of this charm lies a hazier, more complicated story — one of nervy burglary, surreptitious tasks, and the determined quest for unbelievable wealth.

    This account appears as fortune heists — trying and frequently criminal undertakings to purloin important fortunes. These heists, shrouded in interest and secret, have been a common subject in mankind's set of experiences. They rise above times, mainlands, and societies, influencing the records of human progress. Uncovering the tales of these brassy burglaries, Divulging Fortune

Heists: Narratives of Wealth digs into the profundities of the appeal of fortunes and the dull underside of the people who might take extraordinary measures to guarantee them.

Treasure heists are not restricted to the domain of legend or fiction. In our reality, there exist endless unmistakable fortunes, each bearing its own remarkable history, social importance, and persona. These fortunes come in different structures, from the antiquated wealth of Egypt and Rome to the many-sided workmanship bits of the Renaissance, from the lost wealth of wrecks to the relics of tragically missing developments. Every one recounts to a story, a story of creation, social effect, and, here and there, burglary.

Loves frequently overcome any issues between the past and the present, associating us with the civic establishments that preceded. They talk about human creativity, imaginativeness, and the persevering through worth of our aggregate history. In any case, treasures are something other than lifeless things; they are windows into our past, giving experiences into the way of life, social orders, and people who made them. These valuable ancient rarities are demonstrations of the virtuoso of mankind and its capacity to create magnificence and implying that rises above time.

However, as we are attracted to these fortunes, so too are the individuals who might take them. The appeal of riches and the excitement of outfoxing the overseers of social legacy have, from the beginning of time, driven people to plot and execute trying heists. The narratives of these cheats, each with their exceptional inspirations and strategies, are all around as different as the fortunes they look for. From shrewd conmen to sly geniuses, treasure heists have frequently obscured the line among crooks and screw-ups.

The daringness and tricky expected to execute an effective fortune heist couldn't possibly be more significant. These stories of burglary and trick frequently rival the best works of fiction, yet they remain irrefutably genuine, leaving policing, and the overall population excited by the dauntlessness, all things considered, The actual heists, frequently painstakingly arranged and fastidiously executed, keep on testing the restrictions of human creativity and the limits of culpability. The appeal of fortune heists, regardless of their unlawful nature, is profoundly imbued in the human mind. It is established in our interest with the obscure, the unreachable, and the adventure of the pursuit. The mystery and persona encompassing secret fortunes, the legends of old stores and lost privateer gold, mix a base yearning inside us. This yearning for experience and disclosure frequently finds its outlet in the daring universe of fortune heists, where the commitment of riches and the appeal of the obscure are compelling.

The charm of stowed away fortunes likewise fills a subculture of fortune trackers — people who, while not really lawbreakers, are correspondingly attracted to the pursuit. These fortune trackers dare to the profundities of the sea, the remotest corners of the world, and the core of thick woods, directed by legends, bits of hearsay, and verifiable records. Their journeys, filled by a similar hunger for experience and disclosure, frequently obscure the line between real investigation and crime.

The charm of fortune heists, accordingly, brings up significant issues about the human interest with riches and the means by which people will get it. It compels us to contemplate the scarcely discernible difference between real investigation, problematic fortune hunting, and through and through guiltiness. The charm of stowed away wealth drives a few people to the edge of the law, provoking them to leave on hazardous undertakings in quest for their fantasies of untold riches.

Treasure heists, something other than demonstrations of burglary, are naturally attached to the more extensive elements of workmanship, culture, and governmental issues. They frequently act as a focal point through which we can look at these domains. The thought processes behind heists can differ essentially, incorporating a range of individual voracity, patriotism, and, surprisingly, political plans. These heists frequently have repercussions a long ways past the quick demonstration of robbery, undulating through worldwide relations, fights for control, and disagreements regarding proprietorship.

The taken fortunes themselves are changed into political negotiating concessions, and taken workmanship turns into a pawn in worldwide rounds of impact. What was once a workmanship piece or social curio turns into an image of discretionary disunity, a sign of past treacheries, and an impression of present power elements. In this specific circumstance, treasure heists are not just about robbery; they address a burst in the common agreement that keeps countries and social orders intact, testing the actual texture of our common worldwide history.

Treasure heists additionally mirror the more profound human craving to challenge authority, to break liberated from limitations, and to assume command over one's fate. These trying robberies frequently act as a type of resistance, a bid for individual flexibility, or a declaration of personality. The daringness of these activities catches the public's creative mind and accumulates support from the people who feel underestimated or mistreated.

The outcomes of fortune heists arrive at a long ways past the limits of individual demonstrations. They induce an overall manhunt, fuel media furor, and require broad examinations by policing and associations committed to saving social legacy. The most common way of recuperating taken treasures is a story in itself, one where the quest for equity meets the domains of tact and global relations. A lot is on the line, and the difficulties are various, yet the quest for taken loves frequently uncovers the strength of people and associations focused on correcting verifiable wrongs.

Revealing Fortune Heists dives into the universe of craftsmanship phony, investigating the job it plays in both working with and forestalling treasure heists. The appeal of taken cherishes frequently persuades counterfeiters to make reproductions so persuading that they can without much of a stretch delude gatherers, historical centers, and policing. These falsifications add layers of intricacy to the recuperation cycle, as specialists should explore a universe of misdirection to perceive reality.

The universe of fortune heists isn't restricted to a specific time or geological area. All things considered, it traverses the broadness of mankind's set of experiences, including a different exhibit of civilizations and verifiable periods. From the plundering of pharaohs' burial places in old Egypt to the robbery of precious fine arts in present day times, from privateer treasure covered on far off islands to old relics vivacious away by pioneer drives, the universe of fortune heists is both a preview of human desire and an impression of the consistently developing scene of burglary and recuperation.

Revealing Fortune Heists guides perusers on an excursion through time and across mainlands, winding around together the strings of these accounts to introduce a far reaching perspective on the enthralling universe of taken treasures. It investigates the absolute most well known heists ever, from the trying robbery of the Mona Lisa in 1911 to the vanishing of the Russian Golden Room during The Second Great War. Every one of these heists, while novel by its own doing, adds to a bigger story of human desire, interest, and fixation.

Divulging Fortune Heists further uncovers the mind boggling snare of people and associations devoted to saving social legacy and seeking after equity. This people group incorporates archeologists, craftsmanship students of history, examiners, and activists who vigorously work to find taken fortunes and supporter for their re-visitation of their actual owners. Their endeavors, frequently directed in the shadows and across worldwide limits, address the force of assurance and the meaning of protecting our common history.

Generally, the universe of fortune heists is a complex and consistently developing domain, where reality and fiction blend, and the quest for abundance rises above the limits of overall setting. It is a demonstration of the getting through interest with treasures and the dauntlessness of the people who look to have them, even at the expense of overstepping regulations intended to safeguard our social legacy. Through the pages of Divulging Fortune Heists, we uncover the secrets of these bold burglaries, look at their effect on society, and eventually, focus a light on their getting through importance in the fantastic embroidery of mankind's set of experiences.

2. **Setting the stage for the book's exploration**

In the immense embroidery of mankind's set of experiences, there are strings that glimmer with an overwhelming appeal, strings woven from the longing for abundance, the journey for experience, and the unquenchable interest in secret fortunes. These strings have been woven all through the records of progress, forming our reality and making permanent imprints on the aggregate creative mind. The quest for wealth, the charm of the obscure, and the excitement of disclosure have driven individuals to exceptional lengths, starting accounts of fortune that catch the hearts and brains of ages. Inside this complicated story, there exists a specific feature that entices with a tempting interest — a viewpoint that stays in the shadows of desire and fixation: treasure heists.

As we adventure into the investigation of Disclosing Fortune Heists: Narratives of Wealth, making way for our journey is basic. To comprehend the appeal of fortune heists, we should initially dig into the embodiment of fortunes themselves. These fortunes are not simple lifeless things; they are embodied stories, impressions of human creativity, and standards to our common past. They bear the heaviness of civic establishments and the engravings of time, rising above the ages with their excellence, imaginativeness, and social importance.

Treasures come in many structures, each having its extraordinary appeal. From the sparkling pearls of old realms to the complicated craftsmanship bits of the Renaissance, from the relics of tragically missing civilizations to the sea stores concealed underneath the sea's surface, treasures communicate in their very own language. They are the tradition of the pharaohs of Egypt, the wealth of rulers, the creative magnum opuses of painters and stone workers, and the markers of a set of experiences that is both sublime and turbulent. These fortunes hold inside them the virtuoso of humankind, the ability to create magnificence that endures for an extremely long period, and the ageless worth of our aggregate legacy.

However, in their appeal treasures take on an extra aspect. These antiquities span the gap among at various times, permitting us to contact the hands of the people who preceded us and to look into the social orders and people who molded our reality. The interest with treasures rises above overall setting, taking advantage of our major yearning for riches, experience, and the excitement of revelation. A charm stretches out from the profundities of history, where legends of stowed away urban areas of gold and lost privateer accumulates proliferate, to the advanced world, where the commitment of impossible abundance keeps on enrapturing the creative mind.

This charm likewise reaches out to a subculture of fortune trackers who adventure into the obscure, drawn by legends, bits of gossip, and verifiable records. These people, inspired by a similar hunger for experience and revelation, frequently obscure the lines between genuine investigation and the charm of stowed away wealth. They excursion to the farthest reaches of the world, from thick timberlands to far off mountains, in quest for treasures that have evaded others for a really long time. The universe of fortune hunting is one of secret and risk, where the commitment of stowed away wealth entices them into unknown domains.

The charm of fortune heists, spellbinding in its boldness, welcomes us to a universe of venturesome burglary, stealthy tasks, and the people who might take extraordinary measures to guarantee loves that they consider a definitive award. Treasure heists are not bound to the pages of fiction; they are genuine shows that have unfurled over the entire course of time. They are the stories of fortune cheats, driven by their own inspirations, whether filled by private increase, patriotism, or political plans. These cheats, each with their special strategies and reasons, share a typical dauntlessness and shrewd that challenge the constraints of human resourcefulness and the limits of culpability.

The narratives of these trying robberies, a significant number of which are fastidiously arranged and executed, frequently rival the best works of fiction. Nonetheless, they are not show-stoppers; they are true dramatizations that have worked out on the amazing phase of history. The boldness and interest encompassing fortune heists are equipped for charming the public's consideration and testing the best analytical personalities of policing. These stories of burglary and trick frequently leave society awestruck by the daringness and cunning of the crooks in question.

The charm of fortune heists, however grounded in culpability, tracks down a spot in the human mind as an impression of the craving to rock the boat. Treasure heists frequently act as demonstrations of resistance, as offers for individual flexibility, or as affirmations of personality. The dauntlessness of these activities catches the public's creative mind and accumulates support from the individuals who see themselves as underestimated or abused. This appeal, consequently, suggests further conversation starters about our interest with abundance and the lengths to which people will go to get it.

Treasure heists are not detached occasions; they are woven into the texture of mankind's set of experiences and its more extensive elements. These heists frequently have repercussions that stretch out a long ways past the prompt demonstration of robbery, undulating through worldwide relations, battles for control, and disagreements regarding possession. Taken treasures become images of discretionary strife, tokens of past shameful acts, and impressions of present power elements. They are not simply taken craftsmanship or social antiquities; they are vessels of political influence and worldwide debate.

The fallout of fortune heists leads to overall manhunts, media furors, and broad examinations by policing and associations devoted to safeguarding social legacy. The quest for taken treasures is an adventure in itself, one where the quest for equity meets the domains of tact and worldwide relations. The difficulties are various, and a lot is on the line, however the mission to recuperate taken loves frequently uncovers the flexibility of people and associations focused on correcting verifiable wrongs.

Treasure heists likewise converge with the fascinating universe of workmanship imitation, a domain where fake curios are made with such accuracy that they can undoubtedly bamboozle gatherers, exhibition halls, and policing. Counterfeiters, roused by the charm of taken treasures, add a layer of intricacy to the recuperation cycle.

Examiners should explore a snare of trickery to uncover reality, where truth and fiction are entwined, and the genuineness of craftsmanship is a riddle needing settling.

The universe of fortune heists isn't restricted to a specific period or geological area. A domain traverses the broadness of mankind's set of experiences, enveloping different civic establishments and verifiable periods. From the robbery of fortunes from the burial chambers of old pharaohs in Egypt to the plundering of workmanship during the mayhem of battle, from privateer treasures concealed on distant islands to the old relics vivacious away by provincial powers, the universe of fortune heists is a unique material that exhibits human desire, interest, and fixation.

In the pages of Revealing Fortune Heists: Narratives of Wealth, we set out on an excursion through time and across landmasses. We wind around together the strings of these charming stories, introducing a far reaching perspective on the universe of taken treasures and the people who look to recuperate them. Our investigation brings us into the absolute most eminent heists ever, from the trying robbery of the Mona Lisa in 1911 to the disappearing demonstration of the Russian Golden Room during The Second Great War. Every one of these heists, while extraordinary, adds to a bigger story of human desire, interest, and fixation.

As we dig into the accounts of these venturesome burglaries, we uncover that the inspirations driving fortune heists are essentially as different as the actual fortunes. A few cheats are spurred by sheer ravenousness, trying to store up fortunes by selling taken treasures on the underground market. Others carry on of firmly established patriotism, planning to localize social curios they accept were unjustly taken by unfamiliar powers. There are the people who participate in heists as a type of dissent against the foundations they see as oppressors or as a way to cause to notice a specific reason. While their thought processes might contrast, the boldness and clever expected to execute such violations join them in an embroidery of interest and risk.

Divulging Fortune Heists further uncovers the unpredictable organization of people and associations committed to saving social legacy. This people group incorporates archeologists, workmanship students of history, examiners, and activists who commit their lives to finding taken prizes and upholding for their re-visitation of their legitimate spots. Their endeavors are energetic, frequently directed in the shadows, and frequently include cooperation across worldwide lines. Their work addresses the force of assurance and the meaning of defending our common history.

Basically, the universe of fortune heists is a multi-layered and steadily developing domain, where reality and fiction intermix, and the quest for abundance rises above the limits of general setting. It is a demonstration of the persevering through interest with treasures and the daringness of the people who try to have them, even at the expense of violating regulations intended to safeguard our social legacy. Through the pages of Disclosing Fortune Heists, we uncover the secrets of these daring burglaries, look at their effect on society, and at last, focus a light on their getting through importance in the terrific embroidery of mankind's set of experiences.

Chapter 1

The Art of the Heist

The universe of fortune heists is a mind boggling embroidery woven with strings of daringness, clever, and desire. These trying robberies address a dull underside of human interest with riches and the excitement of the unexplored world. However, as we investigate the craft of the heist, it becomes apparent that these lawbreaker tries are something beyond demonstrations of robbery. They are unpredictable tasks, carefully arranged and executed, frequently with a degree of complexity that challenges the actual texture of policing the watchmen of social legacy. The specialty of the heist is a reality where the line among criminal and brains foggy spots, and where the excitement of outfoxing the framework energizes a trying quest for inconceivable wealth.

At the core of the specialty of the heist lies a careful arranging process. Fruitful fortune heists require cautious examination, exact execution, and an unrivaled comprehension of the objective. The hoodlums who set out on these missions frequently commit months, on the off chance that not years, to concentrating on their imprint, distinguishing weaknesses, and creating an arrangement that limits risk while expanding reward. It is a universe of detail and premonition, where each move is a determined move toward a definitive objective.

Research is the foundation of any fortune heist. Lawbreakers should know basically everything there is to know about their objective, grasping its security frameworks, weaknesses, and expected traps. This exploration reaches out to individuals associated with the assurance of the fortune, from security work force to the caretakers of the ancient rarities. In the specialty of the heist, information is power, and the more a crook is familiar with their objective, the better prepared they are to design and execute a fruitful burglary.

This cycle frequently incorporates observation and surveillance. Lawbreakers might invest broad energy noticing the developments of safety faculty, concentrating on designs, and distinguishing flimsy spots. Reconnaissance cameras, cautions, and movement sensors become instruments to be outmaneuvered, and the craft of mixing in and staying subtle is an expertise sharpened flawlessly.

One of the critical components in the specialty of the heist is timing. Hoodlums should distinguish the ideal second to strike, when security is at its generally defenseless. This might include hanging tight for a safety officer's shift change, realizing that a specific caution framework is briefly debilitated, or taking advantage of a second when consideration is redirected somewhere else. The capacity to immediately take advantage of the right chance is urgent to the outcome of the heist.

The arranging stage likewise includes the determination of a group. By and large, heists are not executed by a solitary hoodlum but rather by a group with specific abilities. These groups are frequently made out of people who carry their one of a kind skill to the activity, from safecrackers and hardware experts to falsifiers and skilled accomplices. The cooperative energy between colleagues is urgent, and the progress of a heist frequently depends on successful coordination.

Safety efforts, in the realm of fortune heists, address a test to be survived. From the cutting edge security frameworks of present day exhibition halls and vaults to the multifaceted caution frameworks safeguarding verifiable milestones, lawbreakers face imposing deterrents as they continued looking for treasure. Beating these safety efforts requires sly and expertise as well as mechanical information and the capacity to take advantage of weaknesses in the framework.

Crippling or bypassing alert frameworks, cameras, and movement sensors is a workmanship in itself. It frequently requires a comprehension of gadgets, hacking, or the capacity to take advantage of human mistake. Lawbreakers might utilize different strategies, for example, sticking correspondence frequencies, upsetting power supplies, or controlling security staff for their potential benefit. In the realm of the heist, the capacity to outfox innovation and human reconnaissance is central.

Safecracking, one more component of the specialty of the heist, addresses an expertise that heist groups frequently have. Safes and vaults are intended to be impervious, and the people entrusted with breaking into them should have many-sided information on lock systems and an intense comprehension of strain focuses. It's a fragile dance of accuracy, where the contrast among progress and disappointment can involve milliseconds.

The capacity to stay undetected during a heist is likewise vital to the craftsmanship. Crooks utilize strategies like camouflages, redirection, and confusion to keep security faculty cockeyed and uninformed about their presence. The craft of confusion, specifically, frequently includes making situations that redirect consideration from the heist, whether through arranged episodes, distractions, or astutely positioned baits.

The escape, the last venture in the craft of the heist, is pretty much as essential as the preparation and execution. Crooks should make a perfect departure, escaping seeking after policing coming to a protected place where they can keep out of sight and partake in their not well gotten gains. The escape frequently includes a fastidious arrangement, including get away from courses, transportation, and refuges. The selection of vehicles, courses, and timing are basic variables in an effective departure.

The specialty of the heist additionally reaches out to the removal of taken products. When the fortunes are in the ownership of the hoodlums, they should be covered up, sold, or shipped to where they can be kept securely. This stage frequently includes the utilization of go-betweens, underground organizations, and the formation of bogus personalities to work with the deal or transport of taken craftsmanship. At times, taken treasures stay concealed for quite a long time, once in a while even many years, prior to reemerging.

The boldness of fortune heists lies in their execution as well as in their consequence. When the robbery has happened, the lawbreaker should sidestep catch, discard any proof that could prompt their character, and explore the unpredictable universe of taken craftsmanship and antiquities. Taken fortunes can become prisoners of sorts, as the lawbreaker looks to arrange their return for monetary profit or, at times, political influence.

The underground universe of workmanship and relics burglary is a domain where taken fortunes can change hands on various occasions. Hoodlums might participate in a complicated dance of discussions and exchanges, frequently including global boundaries and a trap of middle people. These delegates, some of the time alluded to as "walls," go about as go betweens who work with the offer of taken merchandise. Now and again, the actual crooks might become craftsmanship sellers, utilizing their insight into the workmanship world to make taken treasures look like genuine acquisitions.

The recuperation of taken craftsmanship and curios is a multi-layered process. It frequently requires the collaboration of policing, social associations, and people committed to saving social legacy. The quest for taken treasures is a worldwide exertion, as examiners follow leads across lines and direction with global accomplices to find the taken relics.

Revealing Fortune Heists likewise investigates the mind boggling universe of craftsmanship falsification, where copies are made with such accuracy that they can undoubtedly misdirect authorities, galleries, and policing. Falsifiers add an additional layer of intricacy to the recuperation interaction, and examiners should depend on their mastery to recognize genuine relics and talented impersonations.

In the craft of the heist, hoodlums and policing participate in a high-stakes mental contest. The quest for taken treasures is an overall undertaking, where specialists utilize each instrument available to them, from measurable investigation and electronic reconnaissance to worldwide joint efforts and covert tasks. The quest for equity unfurls on a worldwide scale, as taken treasures are localized and reestablished to their original owners.

The appeal of fortune heists, in this manner, reaches out past the adventure of the actual burglary. It dives into the complicated universe of arranging, execution, and avoidance, where venturesome hoodlums set their brains in opposition to imposing security frameworks and policing. The craft of the heist is a universe of fastidious examination, cautious timing, and talented cooperation, where everything about and each move can mean the distinction among progress and disappointment.

In the pages of Divulging Fortune Heists, we reveal the narratives of daring robberies and the people who executed them. These stories uncover the complicated snare of arranging, execution, and avoidance that portrays the craft of the heist. As we investigate the universe of taken treasures, we gain knowledge into the mind boggling elements of the underground craftsmanship exchange, the difficulties of recuperation, and the versatility of those committed to saving social legacy. The specialty of the heist, with its boldness and complexity, is a demonstration of the getting through charm of fortunes and the determined quest for unbelievable wealth, even at the expense of violating the regulations intended to safeguard our social legacy. Through these accounts, we gain a more profound comprehension of the mind boggling universe of fortune heists and their getting through importance in the fabulous embroidery of mankind's set of experiences.

1.1 The psychology of heist planning

Behind each effective fortune heist lies an unpredictable trap of brain science, driven by the appeal of abundance, the hunger for experience, and the immovable fixation on secret fortunes. The preparation of a heist is a perplexing interaction that digs profound into the personalities of the individuals who look to outfox security frameworks, dodge policing, hold onto inestimable relics. This unpredictable mental dance is energized by a powerful blend of desire, clever, and the boldness to execute a robbery that challenges the actual texture of lawfulness. To appreciate the brain science of heist arranging, we should take apart the inspirations, the careful examination, the craftiness procedure, and the boldness that support this illegal undertaking.

At the center of heist arranging is the inspiration, a main impetus that constrains people or criminal associations to set out on nervy burglaries. The brain research of inspiration in the domain of fortune heists is multi-layered and frequently perplexing. Monetary profit is a typical inspiration, with hoodlums looking at the likely bonus from selling taken treasures on the bootleg market. The possibility of storing up abundance beyond anything they could ever imagine is a strong temptation that brings numerous into the universe of heist arranging.

Past monetary benefit, patriotism is another inspiration that energizes heist arranging. In certain cases, people and gatherings are driven by a longing to localize social relics that they accept were unjustly taken by unfamiliar powers or pioneer powers. These hoodlums see themselves as bosses of their country's legacy, trying to recover what they view as taken patrimony.

The brain research of inspiration reaches out to the people who participate in heists as a type of dissent or a way to cause to notice a specific reason. These people see robbery for of offering a strong expression, whether it is a dissent against the establishments they see as oppressors or a bid to cause to notice a social or policy centered issue.

Heists with philosophical inspirations frequently obscure the line among culpability and activism, introducing an interesting test to policing examiners.

The specialty of heist arranging is set apart by a comprehensive examination stage that is well established in brain science. Fruitful crooks carefully concentrate on their objectives, learning each complex insight concerning the security frameworks, weaknesses, and people engaged with safeguarding the fortune. The brain science of examination spins around acquiring a top to bottom comprehension of the objective's assets and shortcomings, frequently including an investigation of human brain science.

This examination frequently incorporates observation and surveillance, where hoodlums notice the developments of safety faculty, distinguish designs, and reveal flimsy parts in the security contraption. Reconnaissance cameras, alert frameworks, and movement sensors become

apparatuses to be outmaneuvered, and the capacity to mix into the climate and stay subtle is sharpened flawlessly. Lawbreakers dig into the brain research of safety work force, looking to figure out their schedules, propensities, and expected vulnerable sides.

One of the basic parts of heist arranging is the fastidious timing of the activity. Crooks should distinguish the ideal second to strike, when security is at its generally helpless. The brain science of timing frequently includes sitting tight for a safety officer's shift change, realizing that a specific caution framework is briefly handicapped, or taking advantage of a second when consideration is redirected somewhere else. The brain science of timing stretches out to the comprehension of human way of behaving and brain science, as hoodlums expect and profit by the way of behaving of safety work force.

The arranging stage likewise includes the choice of a group, frequently a group with specific abilities. The brain research of team choice is established in a comprehension of human elements, as heist organizers look for people who supplement each other's assets and shortcomings. Compelling correspondence and trust inside the team are fundamental, just like the capacity to consistently organize and execute the activity.

Safety efforts, in the brain research of heist arranging, address both a test and an open door. Lawbreakers face considerable snags as cutting edge security frameworks, however they additionally see safety efforts as weaknesses to be taken advantage of. The brain science of safety avoidance includes a profound comprehension of innovation, gadgets, and human way of behaving.

The impairing or bypassing of caution frameworks, cameras, and movement sensors addresses a complicated dance of brain science and innovation. Crooks frequently utilize strategies, for example, sticking correspondence frequencies, disturbing power supplies, or controlling security faculty for their potential benefit. The brain research of safety avoidance reaches out to the brain science of human blunder, as hoodlums expect and gain by the missteps that security staff might make.

The specialty of safecracking, one more component in the brain science of heist arranging, requires a significant information on lock systems and an intense comprehension of strain focuses. It is a sensitive dance of accuracy where crooks influence their mental comprehension of safes and vaults to break their guards. The capacity to resist the urge to panic under tension and execute safecracking procedures with accuracy is a demonstration of the mental intuition of heist organizers.

The brain research of heist arranging additionally digs into the idea of staying undetected during the activity. Lawbreakers utilize strategies like camouflages, redirection, and confusion to keep security faculty shaky and ignorant about their presence. The brain science of confusion

frequently includes making situations that redirect consideration from the heist, whether through arranged occurrences, distractions, or astutely positioned baits. Here the organizer expects the responses and ways of behaving of safety faculty.

The escape, the last venture in the brain research of heist arranging, is pretty much as significant as the underlying stages. Crooks should make a spotless departure, evading seeking after policing arriving at a protected place where they can hide out and partake in their not well gotten gains. The brain science of the escape frequently includes a fastidious arrangement, including get away from courses, transportation, and hideaways. It requires a comprehension of human brain research, expecting the activities of policing the responses of the general population.

The specialty of heist arranging likewise reaches out to the removal of taken products, a stage where crooks frequently utilize mediators and underground organizations. The brain research of removal includes the discussion of arrangements, the making of misleading personalities, and a mind boggling comprehension of the underground universe of taken workmanship and curios. Crooks might use their mental information on the craftsmanship world to work with the deal or transport of taken products, frequently concealing them for quite a long time or even many years.

The brain science of heist arranging stretches out to the craft of exchange. When the fortunes are in the ownership of the crooks, they become negotiating tools in a high-stakes round of exchanges. Lawbreakers might utilize their insight into human brain research to arrange the arrival of taken products for monetary benefit or political influence. This stage frequently includes a profound comprehension of human inspirations and the brain science of exchange.

The underground universe of craftsmanship and relics burglary is a domain where taken fortunes can change hands on different occasions. Lawbreakers might take part in complex discussions and exchanges, frequently including global lines and a snare of mediators. These delegates, or "fences," are people who work with the offer of taken merchandise and require a profound comprehension of the brain research of the craftsmanship market and the inspirations of gatherers and purchasers.

The recuperation of taken workmanship and relics is a complex mental undertaking, requiring the participation of policing, social associations, and people committed to saving social legacy. The brain research of recuperation frequently includes the investigation of leads, the following of taken relics across boundaries, and global joint efforts with an accentuation on human brain research.

Uncovering Fortune Heists additionally investigates the mind boggling universe of craftsmanship fabrication, where imitations are made with such accuracy that they can undoubtedly hoodwink authorities, exhibition halls, and policing. Falsifiers add an additional layer of intricacy to the recuperation interaction, and agents should depend on their mental mastery to recognize credible curios and talented impersonations.

The brain science of heist arranging, thusly, is a complex and complicated process that includes inspiration, research, timing, group choice, security avoidance, safe-cracking, brain science of human way of behaving, confusion, the escape, removal, exchange, and recuperation. This brain science is established in an intense comprehension of human way of behaving, the weaknesses of safety frameworks, and the complexities of the underground universe of taken craftsmanship and relics. It is a demonstration of the brain research of desire, tricky, and dauntlessness that drives people and criminal associations to design and execute bold robberies chasing unbelievable riches. Through these accounts, we gain understanding into the perplexing universe of heist arranging and its persevering through importance in the excellent embroidered artwork of mankind's set of experiences.

1.2 Famous heist techniques and tactics

The universe of fortune heists is a domain where nervy robberies are executed with striking accuracy, clever, and key creativity. These well known heists address the zenith of criminal art, with crooks utilizing a bunch of procedures and strategies to outfox security frameworks, policing, the gatekeepers of invaluable fortunes. As we dig into the archives of heist history, we experience stories that exhibit the boldness of human desire and the brain science of robbery, disclosing the methods and strategies that have made permanent imprints on the universe of wrongdoing.

Quite possibly of the most notorious procedure utilized in heists is the craft of mask. Lawbreakers have, over and over, depended on masks to penetrate their objective, mix in with the climate, and avoid recognition. Whether it's wearing the regalia of safety faculty, acting like support laborers, or taking on the appearance of gallery staff, masks are a flexible and fundamental device in the heist organizer's munitions stockpile. This procedure not just permits hoodlums to get close enough to limited regions yet additionally gives a chance to concentrate on security faculty and their schedules.

The venturesome burglary of the Mona Lisa from the Louver in 1911 fills in as a model of this procedure. Vincenzo Peruggia, an Italian jack of all trades and painter, masked himself as a Louver worker to conceal inside the historical center for the time being. Once covered, he jumping all over the chance to eliminate the amazingly popular canvas from its casing and hide it underneath his dress. Peruggia's effective mask permitted him to stay inconspicuous until he had made his getaway with the precious show-stopper.

Taking advantage of interruptions and redirections is one more strategy every now and again utilized in heists. Hoodlums make aggravations or occasions intended to distract from the robbery, redirecting security staff and policing their essential goal. These redirections can take many structures, from arranged occurrences like flames or mishaps to intentional interruptions intended to plant disarray and confusion. The progress of this strategy depends on the capacity to control human brain research and conduct.

The Isabella Stewart Gardner Historical center heist of 1990 gives an illustrative illustration of redirection strategies. Two cheats masked as cops showed up at the exhibition hall's entry, professing to answer a detailed unsettling influence. While one of them kept the security staff involved in one piece of the gallery, the other utilized the interruption to get to the displays and take a few important fine arts. The organized unsettling influence redirected consideration from the robbery, permitting the cheats to get away from before the real essence of the occurrence was found.

Lawbreakers likewise utilize the procedure of taking advantage of primary weaknesses in their heist plans. By recognizing shortcomings in a structure's engineering or security frameworks, they can get close enough to their objectives all the more without any problem. This could include getting to ventilation conduits, unfinished plumbing spaces, or in any event, burrowing into the premises from a nearby structure. Understanding the weaknesses of the actual climate is an essential part of heist arranging.

The nervy bank heist in Stockholm in 1973, regularly alluded to as the "Norrmalmstorg Burglary," gives an instance of taking advantage of underlying weaknesses. The hoodlums leased a loft that common a wall with the bank's vault. North of a while, they penetrated a passage through the wall and effectively penetrated the bank's vault. The underlying shortcoming of the structure was their key to an effective heist.

Profoundly refined strategies for bypassing security frameworks, like alerts and cameras, are indispensable to many heists. Lawbreakers frequently utilize their specialized mastery to impair or stick caution frameworks, slice capacity to surveillance cameras, or take advantage of correspondence weaknesses. These strategies require a profound comprehension of hardware and the capacity to outfox state of the art innovation.

The Hatton Nursery heist in London in 2015 fills in to act as an illustration of taking advantage of safety frameworks. A gathering of old hoodlums, known as the "Terrible Granddads," debilitated the caution arrangement of the Hatton Nursery Safe Store Organization and penetrated into the vault to get to its items. Their mastery in impairing current security innovation permitted them to do the daring burglary undetected.

Brain science assumes a critical part in many heists, as crooks control the way of behaving and feelings of those required, from security faculty to policing. Mental strategies might include taking advantage of human shortcomings, like insatiability, dread, or trust. At times, hoodlums make a need to keep moving or disarray to provoke silly reactions from their objectives.

The Incomparable Train Burglary of 1963, a well known heist in the Unified Realm, features the utilization of brain science in criminal strategies. The posse fastidiously arranged the burglary of a Regal Mail train conveying money and resources. They controlled the train's flagging framework to make it stop, then, at that point, compromised the train group with savagery. By making a need to get moving and dread, the hoodlums incited the team to coordinate, empowering them to hold onto the train's significant freight.

The utilization of insider data and agreement with people working at the objective area is one more method ordinarily utilized in heists. This approach permits hoodlums to acquire personal information on security conventions, access codes, and the design of the premises. Insiders can either be pressured into supporting the heist or may eagerly take an interest for a portion of the taken plunder.

The trying burglary of the Isabella Stewart Gardner Historical center in 1990, recently referenced for its redirection strategies, additionally elaborate an insider. A safety officer at the exhibition hall, Richard Abath, was found to have permitted the cheats admittance to the premises. Abath professed to be an accidental member, yet his plot with the lawbreakers assumed a significant part in the outcome of the heist.

The brain science of control stretches out to the domain of workmanship phony. Crooks frequently make fake fine arts or antiques with such accuracy that they can undoubtedly misdirect gatherers, exhibition halls, and policing. This strategy includes taking advantage of the brain research of specialists, craftsmanship specialists, and organizations that depend on visual investigation and provenance to confirm workmanship.

The instance of Han van Meegeren, a Dutch workmanship counterfeiter dynamic during and after The Second Great War, represents this strategy. Van Meegeren delivered fake masterpieces in the style of Dutch Brilliant Age aces like Johannes Vermeer. His phonies were persuading to such an extent that they tricked craftsmanship specialists and gatherers. Van Meegeren took advantage of the brain research of epicureans who accepted they were obtaining certified Vermeers, and he figured out how to sell his frauds at exorbitant costs.

Hoodlums may likewise utilize the strategy of long haul arranging, committing months or even a very long time to concentrating on their objective, grasping its weaknesses, and making a heist plan that limits risk while boosting reward. This degree of responsibility and persistence is an essential part of heist strategies, permitting lawbreakers to take advantage of their objectives when they are least ready.

The trying robbery of the Banco Focal in Fortaleza, Brazil, in 2005 fills in to act as an illustration of long haul arranging. A gathering of criminals endured three months digging a passage from a leased property to the bank's vault. The passage, which was in excess of 78 meters in length, empowered them to get to the vault. The dauntlessness of the arrangement and the obligation to long stretches of work concentrated work represent the utilization of long haul arranging as a heist strategy.

The fallout of heists frequently includes the strategy of exchange. Taken treasures become negotiating advantages, and lawbreakers might utilize their insight into the workmanship world, the brain research of authorities, and the inspirations of purchasers to arrange the arrival of taken merchandise for monetary profit or political influence. Exchange is a mind boggling and sensitive cycle, requiring a comprehension of human brain research and the elements of the underground workmanship exchange.

The venturesome burglary of Edward Chomp's notorious painting, "The Shout," in 1994 gives an illustrative illustration of discussion strategies. The lawbreakers, mindful of the worth and social meaning of the work of art, started dealings with Norwegian experts for its return. The brain research of discussion included a cautious harmony between monetary profit and the longing for public acknowledgment. The composition was in the long run recuperated, and the exchanges shed light on the mind boggling brain research of craftsmanship robbery and recuperation.

The universe of fortune heists is packed with popular cases that exhibit the bold procedures and strategies utilized by hoodlums to accomplish their goals. These strategies range from the utilization of masks and redirections to taking advantage of primary weaknesses, controlling security situation, and utilizing mental control. Insider conspiracy, long haul arranging, and the craft of exchange are likewise necessary parts of heist strategies. Through these accounts, we gain understanding into the dynamic and diverse universe of heist procedures and strategies, where nervy crooks take part in a high-stakes round of methodology and deception, testing the best personalities of policing security. These heists are a demonstration of the persevering through charm of fortunes and the constant quest for incredible wealth, even at the expense of overstepping the regulations intended to safeguard our social legacy.

1.3 The cat-and-mouse game with law enforcement

In the shadowy universe of fortune heists, a perplexing wait-and-see game unfurls, one that sets nervy crooks in opposition to the tireless assurance of policing. The quest for taken treasures addresses a high-stakes challenge, where examiners, analysts, and organizations entrusted with recuperating precious relics participate in an extended clash of brains with the people who try to outfox the framework. This continuous battle uncovers a perplexing interchange of procedure, clever, and the tenacious quest for equity, enlightening the waiting game that characterizes the universe of fortune heists.

Policing, from nearby police divisions to specific units, are entrusted with the stupendous test of safeguarding social legacy and recuperating taken treasures. The quest for equity frequently starts with the underlying reaction to a heist, where examiners are called to the scene to survey what is going on, accumulate proof, and recognize leads. This beginning stage of the wait-and-see game is basic in deciding the course and progress of the examination.

Proof assortment is a basic part of the insightful interaction. Criminal investigators should carefully record the crime location, gathering actual proof like fingerprints, DNA, and reconnaissance film. The brain research of proof assortment is established in meticulousness, tender loving care, and the use of logical strategies to distinguish possible leads. The capacity to decipher the pieces of information abandoned by law-breakers is key to the analytical cycle.

Now and again, policing utilize specific units or teams committed to craftsmanship and ancient pieces wrongdoing. These units carry a novel arrangement of abilities to the wait-and-see game, with skill in workmanship history, social legacy, and the complexities of the craftsmanship market. Their insight is instrumental in recognizing taken treasures, finding leads, and working together with worldwide accomplices.

The trading of data and cooperation among policing are essential parts of the wait-and-see game. Taken loves frequently cross lines, making worldwide collaboration a need. Analysts and examiners should explore complex lawful and administrative difficulties to share data and direction endeavors. This joint effort stretches out to INTERPOL, which assumes a fundamental part in working with the trading of data on taken social property.

Interpol's Taken Masterpieces data set is a significant asset in the battle against workmanship robbery. It furnishes policing with a stage to share data about taken craftsmanship and curios, empowering investigators to cross-reference things with the information base to recognize taken pieces and find leads. The data set is a demonstration of the worldwide size of the wait-and-see game, where examiners depend on global organizations to recuperate taken treasures.

The wait-and-see game additionally includes the brain research of profiling and figuring out the psyche of the lawbreaker. Criminal investigators should dissect the thought processes and conduct of cheats, utilizing mental experiences to foresee their best courses of action. Profiling methods frequently dig into the brain science of aspiration, voracity, and the longing for acknowledgment, assisting examiners with expecting the activities of hoodlums.

The examination of taken cherishes frequently prompts a trap of underground organizations, where taken curios change hands on numerous occasions. Hoodlums and walls explore the complex universe of the underground market, utilizing strategies to wash the beginnings of taken things. Analysts should penetrate these organizations, acting like possible purchasers or venders to accumulate data and find leads.

One of the striking parts of the wait-and-see game with policing the utilization of sources. Insiders inside the criminal world or those with information on taken fortunes can give basic data to specialists. These people might help out policing different reasons, like looking for decreased sentences or monetary prizes. The utilization of witnesses is a sensitive strategy, requiring an equilibrium between trust and watchfulness.

An emotional illustration of source use chasing taken treasures is the situation of the taken Isabella Stewart Gardner Historical center fine arts. In 1990, a Boston criminal, Carmine Romano, gave data about the taken craftsmanship to the FBI. The data at last prompted the recognizable proof of the hoodlums and the recuperation of a portion of the taken pieces. The utilization of sources was critical in this high-profile case and embodies the complex strategies utilized in the waiting game.

The waiting game additionally delves into the domain of mechanical progressions. As crooks become more complex, policing should adjust by utilizing state of the art innovation in their examinations. Procedures like criminological examination, computerized following, and facial acknowledgment programming have become basic devices chasing after equity. These mechanical advances are an impression of the developing idea of the waiting game, where investigators embrace advancement to remain on the ball.

The recuperation of taken workmanship and ancient rarities frequently includes the strategy of goading, where policing traps or uses spies to captivate lawbreakers into compromising circumstances. This strategy requires a profound comprehension of criminal way of behaving and brain research, as investigators expect the activities of those looking to procure taken merchandise. The utilization of teasing is an essential move intended to prompt the misgiving of hoodlums.

The waiting game additionally extends to the fight in court to localize taken treasures. Examinations frequently uncover the presence of taken antiquities in the ownership of gatherers, exhibition halls, or foundations. The lawful course of recuperating these things can be extended and complex, including talks, legitimate cases, and peaceful accords. The quest for equity in the lawful field addresses an alternate feature of the wait-and-see game.

Compensation claims, which try to return taken relics to their legitimate owners or nations of beginning, are a huge part of the fight in court. These cases are established in the brain research of social legacy and the ethical basic to right authentic wrongs. The legitimate cycle includes introducing proof of robbery, possession, and the conditions encompassing the plundering or burglary of social property.

One of the most popular fights in court for bringing home is the situation of the Elgin Marbles, otherwise called the Parthenon Marbles. These old Greek models were taken out from the Parthenon in Athens by Master Elgin in the mid nineteenth hundred years and are presently housed in the English Gallery. Greece has long looked for their return, and the lawful and strategic endeavors to localize the marbles epitomize the complexities of the wait-and-see game in the legitimate field.

The wait-and-see game isn't bound to the universe of policing. Confidential people, activists, and associations devoted to social legacy conservation are basic players chasing after taken treasures. Their endeavors are eager and frequently directed in the shadows, as they work to find taken ancient rarities and supporter for their re-visitation of their legitimate spots.

Social associations, like UNESCO, assume a huge part in the worldwide fight against craftsmanship burglary. UNESCO's Show on the Method for Disallowing and Forestalling the Illegal Import, Product and Move of Responsibility for Property fills in as a foundation of worldwide endeavors to safeguard social legacy. The show gives a legitimate system to the compensation of taken social property and the counteraction of its unlawful exchange.

The getting through meaning of the waiting game lies in its capacity to reveal the complicated organization of people and associations committed to protecting social legacy. It is a demonstration of the force of assurance and the meaning of protecting our common history. The waiting game is a dynamic and consistently developing fight, where daring hoodlums challenge the best personalities in policing, tireless quest for equity crosses global lines, and the brain research of burglary and recuperation shapes the course of history.

The universe of fortune heists is a multi-layered domain, where reality and fiction intermix, and the quest for equity rises above the limits of overall setting. It is a demonstration of the persevering through interest with treasures and the steadfast obligation to their insurance. Through these accounts, we gain understanding into the complex and developing wait-and-see

game that describes the universe of fortune heists, where the venturesome desires of crooks are met with the tenacious assurance of those devoted to maintaining the law and saving our social legacy.

Chapter 2

Masterminds of Audacity

The universe of fortune heists is a domain populated by an interesting cast of characters, some of whom have procured the title of "geniuses" for their nervy endeavors. These people or criminal associations are the engineers of fastidiously arranged and trying heists that have enthralled the public's creative mind and perplexed policing. They are driven by aspiration, clever, and an immovable craving for incredible abundance. This investigation brings us into the personalities of these driving forces of dauntlessness, revealing insight into their inspirations, techniques, and the getting through appeal of fortune heists.

Spurred by the longing for wealth, brains of daringness frequently have a voracious hunger for abundance. Their brassy heists are powered by the possibility of gathering untold fortunes, driving them to focus on a portion of the world's most important fortunes. Their dauntlessness lies in the actual burglary as well as in the fastidious preparation, sly methodology, and impeccable execution expected to outmaneuver the imposing security frameworks intended to safeguard these fortunes.

Quite possibly of the most notorious figure in the realm of fortune heists is Leonardo Notarbartolo, the genius behind the brassy burglary of the Banco Focal in Fortaleza, Brazil, in 2005. Notarbartolo, an Italian hoodlum with a background marked by brassy heists, organized an arrangement to invade the bank's vault through an underground passage. This venturesome plan required a very long time of careful preparation and the participation of a group of accessories. The criminals effectively got to the vault and grabbed an expected $70 million worth of money and resources.

Notarbartolo's daringness was not restricted to the actual heist but rather likewise reached out to his utilization of confusion and the production of bogus prompts redirect policing. He established signs and manufactured proof, leaving examiners in a mess and vulnerability. His dauntlessness lay in his capacity to outfox both the bank's security frameworks and the ensuing examination, all in quest for untold abundance.

While monetary benefit is an intense inspiration for some brains of boldness, some are driven by patriotism, philosophy, or individual feuds. These people might consider their heists to be demonstrations of retaliation or as a way to cause to notice social or political causes. The daringness in such cases isn't exclusively in that frame of mind of abundance however in the longing to offer a striking expression and rock the boat.

In 1974, a gathering of activists took The Stone of Scone, an image of Scottish patriotism, from Westminster Monastery in London. Their bold demonstration was a dissent contrary to English rule and the concealment of Scottish character. The boldness lay in their eagerness to challenge the English foundation and the representative meaning of the stone. While the stone was at last recuperated and returned, the brassy burglary prevailed with regards to causing to notice the reason and stirring help for Scottish autonomy.

The brain science of geniuses of boldness is an intricate interaction of desire, clever, and the daringness to challenge the framework. These people have an interesting mix of insight, creativity, and resolute assurance. Their boldness is clear in their capacity to consider and execute heists that resist the chances and enamor the public's creative mind.

Driving forces of daringness are much of the time portrayed by their careful preparation and vital virtuoso. These bold heists require cautious examination, exact execution, and a profound comprehension of the objective. The lawbreakers who organize them devote critical time and assets to concentrating on their imprint, distinguishing weaknesses, and making plans that limit risk while expanding reward. The boldness lies in the burglary as well as in the intricate planning that goes before it.

The boldness of arranging is exemplified by the daring heist of the Isabella Stewart Gardner Historical center in 1990. Two criminals camouflaged as cops acquired passage to the exhibition hall and took thirteen significant craftsmanships, including works of art by Vermeer, Rembrandt, and Degas. The boldness of the arrangement included camouflages, redirection, and careful observation. The criminals had concentrated on the gallery's design, security frameworks, and schedules of the staff. Their dauntlessness was not restricted to the actual robbery but rather additionally stretched out to the complicated arranging that empowered them to hold onto the precious works of art.

Timing is a basic component in the boldness of heist arranging. Crooks should distinguish the ideal second to strike, when security is at its generally defenseless. This might include hanging tight for a safety officer's shift change, realizing that a specific caution framework is briefly impaired, or taking advantage of a second when consideration is redirected somewhere else. The dauntlessness lies in jumping all over the right chance, frequently with split-second accuracy.

The boldness of timing is highlighted by the nervy burglary of the Incomparable Train Theft in 1963. The pack carefully arranged the burglary of a Regal Mail train conveying money and resources. They controlled the train's flagging framework to make it stop, then, at that point, undermined the train group with viciousness. By making a need to keep moving and dread, the lawbreakers incited the group to participate, empowering them to hold onto the train's significant freight.

The daringness of arranging likewise includes the choice of a group. By and large, heists are not executed by a solitary hoodlum but rather by a group with particular abilities. These groups are frequently made out of people who carry their extraordinary aptitude to the activity, from safecrackers and gadgets experts to counterfeiters and skilled accomplices. The cooperative energy between colleagues is significant, and the boldness of a fruitful heist frequently depends on powerful coordination.

The daringness of safety avoidance is one more sign of driving forces of dauntlessness. Security frameworks, whether exceptional alert frameworks, reconnaissance cameras, or movement sensors, address impressive deterrents to burglary. Effectively outfoxing these frameworks requires a profound comprehension of innovation, gadgets, and human way of behaving. Hoodlums should handicap or sidestep safety efforts to get to their objective.

The boldness of safety avoidance is clear in the venturesome Hatton Nursery heist in London in 2015. A gathering of older hoodlums, known as the "Terrible Grand-dads," crippled the caution arrangement of the Hatton Nursery Safe Store Organization and bored into the vault to get to its items. Their ability in impairing current security innovation permitted them to do the daring robbery undetected.

Safecracking is a workmanship that requires a significant information on lock systems and an intense comprehension of strain focuses. The dauntlessness of safecracking lies in the capacity to resist the urge to panic under tension and execute strategies with accuracy. It is a sensitive dance of expertise and mental keenness, as safecrackers control locks to break their guards.

The bold robbery of the Banco Focal in Fortaleza, Brazil, gives an instance of safecracking as a critical component of the dauntlessness. The criminals penetrated through the vault's walls to get to the items, a fastidious and in fact requesting task. Their boldness was in the penetration of the vault as well as in the dominance of safecracking procedures that empowered them to get to the money and resources inside.

The daringness of heist arranging reaches out to the brain research of human way of behaving. Crooks expect the activities of safety faculty and control their way of behaving for their potential benefit. Whether through redirection, confusion, or terrorizing, geniuses of daringness comprehend the brain science of the people who hold them up and utilize it for their potential benefit.

The venturesome Isabella Stewart Gardner Gallery heist in 1990 involved the control of human brain science. The hoodlums acted like cops, making a misguided feeling of power that prompted the consistence of the exhibition hall's security faculty. Their boldness was in their capacity to take advantage of the trust and participation of those answerable for safeguarding the extremely valuable fine arts.

Confusion is a method much of the time utilized by brains of boldness. Crooks make situations that redirect consideration from the heist, frequently through arranged episodes, distractions, or keenly positioned fakes. The dauntlessness of confusion includes making disarray and disorder to keep security faculty reeling and ignorant about the burglary.

The boldness of confusion is exemplified by the brassy robbery of the Banco Focal in Fortaleza, Brazil. The criminals established explosives in a vacant part close to the bank, making a gigantic blast that redirected policing specialists on call. The bedlam and disarray coming about because of the blast permitted the hoodlums to do the venturesome heist while specialists were engrossed with the occurrence.

The dauntlessness of the escape is essentially as critical as the underlying phases of a heist. Crooks should make a perfect departure, escaping seeking after policing arriving at a protected place where they can disappear and partake in their poorly gotten gains. The brain science of the escape includes a comprehension of human way of behaving, expecting the activities of policing the responses of people in general.

The boldness of the escape is featured in the nervy Hatton Nursery heist. After effectively penetrating the vault, the cheats confronted the test of getting away with their plunder. They made their escape in a van, yet their boldness stretched out to the utilization of a decisively left vehicle that hindered the entry to the road. This strategy was intended to dial back any chasing after policing purchase the hoodlums essential opportunity to arrive at their hideaway.

The venturesome burglary of Edward Chomp's notable painting, "The Shout," in 1994 gives an illustrative illustration of discussion strategies. The lawbreakers started discussions with Norwegian experts for the arrival of the composition, utilizing the brain research of monetary benefit and the craving for public acknowledgment. The boldness of discussion was in their capacity to haggle with policing the arrival of the taken show-stopper.

The universe of fortune heists is loaded with geniuses of dauntlessness who have the insight, creativity, and enduring assurance to execute brassy heists. These brassy crooks challenge the best personalities in policing security, pushing the limits of what is conceivable chasing riches and acknowledgment.

The brain science of geniuses of dauntlessness dives profound into the many-sided inspirations, arranging, and execution of their heists. Their dauntlessness is a demonstration of the persevering through charm of fortunes and the steady quest for incomprehensible wealth, even at the expense of overstepping the regulations intended to safeguard our social legacy. Through these accounts, we gain knowledge into the complex and always developing universe of daring heists, where the dauntlessness of crooks is met with the tireless assurance of those devoted to maintaining the law and safeguarding our social legacy.

2.1 Detailed profiles of notorious heist masterminds

The universe of famous heist driving forces is a spellbinding domain populated by people who have exhibited venturesome desire, key virtuoso, and relentless assurance in their quest for unfathomable wealth. These geniuses have become legends in the records of wrongdoing, organizing probably the most daring and carefully arranged heists ever. In this investigation, we dive into itemized profiles of a limited handful of these famous figures, revealing insight into their experiences, inspirations, strategies, and the persevering through interest that encompasses them.

1. **Leonardo Notarbartolo**
   Foundation:
   Leonardo Notarbartolo, an Italian criminal, is maybe most popular for engineering the venturesome robbery of the Banco Focal in Fortaleza, Brazil, in 2005. Before this infamous heist, Notarbartolo had a broad lawbreaker record, which incorporated a background marked by bold robberies and thefts. His standing for tricky and dauntlessness went before him, and his mastery in arranging and executing complex heists made him an imposing figure in the realm of wrongdoing.

   Inspiration:
   Notarbartolo's inspiration was essentially monetary. He was driven by the craving for gigantic riches and was able to put huge time and assets in arranging brassy heists to accomplish his objective. The daring heist of the Banco Focal was a chance to store up an expected $70 million worth of money and resources, an award that was excessively enticing for Notarbartolo to stand up to.

   Daring Heist:
   The daring robbery of the Banco Focal involved invading the bank's vault through a carefully dug underground passage. Notarbartolo and his group went through months arranging and executing the heist, an accomplishment that necessary a profound comprehension of safecracking and the underlying weaknesses of the structure. Their boldness lay in the intricate preparation, execution, and the capacity to outmaneuver impressive security frameworks.

   Capers:
   After the brassy heist, Notarbartolo's dauntlessness stretched out to his utilization of confusion and making misleading prompts redirect policing. He established hints and manufactured proof, leaving examiners in a mess and vulnerability. His capacity to make redirections and sow disorder exhibited his unmatched daringness in testing the specialists.

2. **The Pink Pumas**
   Foundation:
   The Pink Jaguars are an infamous global organization of gem criminals known for their bold heists and careful preparation. The gathering is made out of people from different nations, fundamentally from the Balkans. Their name gets from their utilization of pink-hued dress and frill as camouflages during their heists. Their dauntlessness has procured them a spot in the records of present day heist legends.

Inspiration:

The Pink Jaguars are principally propelled by monetary benefit. They target top of the line adornments stores, frequently in glitzy urban communities, and grab a large number of dollars worth of jewels and other valuable gemstones. Their daringness lies in their capacity to penetrate vigorously strengthened stores and getaway with their plunder.

Nervy Heists:

The Pink Pumas' venturesome heists incorporate the robbery of the Thousand years Star jewel, a 203.04-carat diamond, from the Thousand years Vault in London in 2000. The daringness of this robbery was in their capacity to outsmart security frameworks and getaway with one of the world's most significant precious stones. Their heists frequently include crushing showcase cases, exhibiting their dauntless way to deal with robbery.

Ventures:

The Pink Pumas' daringness reaches out to their capacity to avoid policing global lines. They have been engaged with heists in various nations, and their utilization of masks, speedy excursions, and a complicated organization of contacts has permitted them to stay on the loose for broadened periods. Their daringness isn't just in the actual robbery yet in their capacity to explore the worldwide policing.

3. **Valerio Viccei**

Foundation:

Valerio Viccei was an Italian genius who became scandalous for organizing the brassy and shameless heist of the Knightsbridge Safe Store Community in London in 1987. Before his contribution in this famous heist, Viccei was at that point a carefully prepared criminal with a background marked by bold thefts and outfitted bank heists. His standing for daringness and shrewd made him an impressive figure in the criminal hidden world.

Inspiration:

Viccei's essential inspiration was monetary benefit. He considered the Knightsbridge heist to be a valuable chance to accumulate a huge fortune by taking the items in high-security wellbeing store boxes. His dauntlessness lay in his readiness to assume the considerable test of breaking into quite possibly of London's most protected vault.

Venturesome Heist:

The venturesome heist of the Knightsbridge Safe Store Place included the utilization of guns to stifle staff and security faculty. Viccei and his accessories then, at that point, continued to break into the wellbeing store boxes, grabbing an expected £60 million worth of money, gems, and different resources. The dauntlessness of the heist was in the utilization of weapons and the capacity to outsmart security.

Capers:

Viccei's daringness stretched out to his departure plan. He escaped to Latin America, where he resided as an outlaw for a considerable length of time. His capacity to evade policing avoid catch displayed his venturesome methodology not exclusively to the heist yet additionally to the consequence and break.

4. **The Thomas Crown Pack**

Foundation:

The Thomas Crown Pack, named after the imaginary person Thomas Crown from the 1968 film "The Thomas Crown Undertaking," is a gathering of brassy workmanship hoodlums known for taking significant compositions and curios. This criminal association is accepted to have been dynamic for a very long time, with individuals beginning from various nations. Their daringness and careful arranging have made them famous figures in the realm of workmanship robbery.

Inspiration:

The Thomas Crown Posse's essential inspiration is monetary profit through the robbery and ensuing offer of important works of art. Their daringness lies in their capacity to enter historical centers, exhibitions, and confidential assortments to grab precious fortunes.

Bold Heists:

The bold heists organized by the Thomas Crown Group incorporate the robbery of the notable work of art "The Madonna of the Yarnwinder" by Leonardo da Vinci in 2003. The daringness of this heist was in their capacity to penetrate a Scottish palace and take a work of art esteemed at a large number of dollars. Their bold heists frequently include masks, redirection, and careful preparation.

Ventures:

The Thomas Crown Pack's boldness reaches out to their capacity to stay on the loose for broadened periods. Their individuals are known to have utilized bogus personalities, made underground organizations, and utilized middle people to work with the offer of taken craftsmanship. Their boldness isn't just in the heist yet in their capacity to explore the complicated and clandestine universe of taken craftsmanship and relics.

5. **Carl Gugasian**

Foundation:

Carl Gugasian, otherwise called the "Friday Night Bank looter," is an American genius who became famous for organizing a line of venturesome bank burglaries in the last part of the 1990s and mid 2000s. Gugasian had no lawbreaker record prior to setting out on his brassy heist binge, making his progress into a driving force significantly more surprising.

Inspiration:

Gugasian's inspiration was principally monetary. His daringness lay in his capacity to change from a decent resident to a driving force who fastidiously arranged and executed a progression of venturesome bank heists to store up riches. His inspiration was pull in the craving for monetary security and freedom.

Brassy Heists:

The brassy heists organized by Gugasian involved the invasion of different banks, frequently late on a Friday night, when security staff were diminished. His boldness was clear in his capacity to outsmart security frameworks, incapacitate alerts, and departure without abandoning any hint of his personality. He utilized different masks and redirection strategies to befuddle observers and examiners.

Ventures:

Gugasian's dauntlessness reached out to his capacity to stay unidentified for a drawn out period, notwithstanding a line of high-profile heists. His utilization of misleading characters, hermetically sealed vindications, and fastidious arranging permitted him to sidestep policing an extensive time. The daringness of his heists was in the execution as well as in his capacity to evade catch.

These point by point profiles of infamous heist driving forces shed light on the people and criminal associations that have made brassy heists a piece of their criminal heritage. Their inspirations, nervy heists, and capers grandstand the broadness of human desire, crafty, and the steadfast assurance to accomplish inconceivable riches. These brains have made a permanent imprint on the universe of wrongdoing, testing policing security frameworks with their boldness and fastidious preparation. The getting through interest with their accounts features the immortal charm of fortune heists and the unyielding soul of the individuals who arrange them.

2.2 Their motivations, personalities, and criminal careers

Famous heist driving forces come from different foundations, showing a great many inspirations, characters, and criminal vocations. These people or criminal associations have made a permanent imprint on the universe of wrongdoing through their nervy endeavors. In this investigation, we dive into their inspirations, characters, and criminal professions, revealing insight into the perplexing elements that drive them to coordinate nervy heists.

1. **Leonardo Notarbartolo**

   Inspiration:

   Leonardo Notarbartolo's essential inspiration was monetary benefit. He was driven by a voracious longing for riches and was able to put broad time and assets in arranging bold heists to accomplish this objective. Notarbartolo's daringness was established in the possibility of storing up gigantic abundance by organizing fastidiously arranged heists, like the robbery of the Banco Focal in Fortaleza, Brazil.

   Character:

Notarbartolo had a few character qualities that made him a fruitful heist plan. He exhibited knowledge, creativity, and steadfast assurance. His capacity to design and execute complex heists, as well as his dauntlessness in confronting impressive security frameworks, exhibited his assurance to accomplish his objectives.

Criminal Profession:

Notarbartolo had a broad lawbreaker profession set apart by bold robberies and thefts. He acquired a standing for clever and daringness, which went before his contribution in the famous heist of the Banco Focal. His crook vocation showed his mastery in arranging and executing complex heists, solidifying his status as an imposing figure in the realm of wrongdoing.

2. **The Pink Jaguars**

Inspiration:

The Pink Pumas' essential inspiration is monetary profit through the burglary and ensuing offer of significant gems. Their daringness is driven by the possibility of accumulating a huge number of dollars worth of jewels and valuable gemstones. The daringness of the Pink Jaguars lies in their eagerness to target very good quality adornments stores, frequently in fabulous urban communities, and grab their important plunder.

Character:

The Pink Jaguars, as a criminal association, display a scope of characters among their individuals. These people are clever, versatile, and ready to function as a component of a group. Their daringness is supported by their capacity to design and execute heists in an exceptionally organized way. They show a daring way to deal with burglary and avoidance of policing.

Criminal Vocation:

The Pink Jaguars have a long and celebrated criminal profession, set apart by a progression of nervy heists. Their individuals come from different nations and are known for their careful preparation and execution. The boldness of their heists frequently includes crushing presentation cases and outsmarting security frameworks, showing their cleverness and assurance in the realm of gems burglary.

3. **Valerio Viccei**

Inspiration:

Valerio Viccei's essential inspiration was monetary benefit through the burglary of significant things from security store boxes. The boldness of his heist at the Knightsbridge Safe Store Community was driven by the possibility of gathering gigantic riches. Viccei considered this nervy heist to be a chance to accomplish monetary security and freedom.

Character:

Viccei showed a scope of character qualities that added to his prosperity as a driving force. He was known for his daringness, knowledge, and creativity. His progress from a decent resident to a driving force who carefully arranged and executed a progression of bold heists displayed his assurance and versatility.

Criminal Profession:

Before his contribution in the famous Knightsbridge heist, Valerio Viccei had a lawbreaker vocation set apart by brassy burglaries and furnished bank heists. His dauntlessness and clever made him an imposing figure in the criminal hidden world. The boldness of the Knightsbridge heist was in his capacity to repress security faculty, incapacitate cautions, and break with an expected £60 million worth of money, adornments, and assets.

4. **The Thomas Crown Group**

Inspiration:

The Thomas Crown Group's essential inspiration is monetary profit through the robbery and ensuing offer of significant fine arts. Their boldness is driven by the amazing chance to penetrate exhibition halls, displays, and confidential assortments to snatch invaluable fortunes. The daringness of their heists frequently includes camouflages, redirection, and fastidious preparation.

Character:

The individuals from the Thomas Crown Posse show a scope of characters inside the criminal association. They are clever, versatile, and fit for cooperating in a planned way. Their dauntlessness is supported by their capacity to design and execute complex heists, frequently including the burglary of extremely valuable workmanship and antiquities.

Criminal Profession:

The Thomas Crown Posse is accepted to have been dynamic for a considerable length of time, with individuals beginning from various nations. Their brassy heists have made them famous figures in the realm of workmanship burglary. The dauntlessness of their heists frequently includes the utilization of masks and redirection strategies, displaying their fastidious preparation and execution.

5. **Carl Gugasian**

Inspiration:

Carl Gugasian's essential inspiration was monetary profit. His dauntlessness was established in the possibility of hoarding abundance through a progression of nervy bank burglaries. Gugasian looked for monetary security and freedom through his crook takes advantage of, making an emotional progress from an honest resident to a brains.

Character:

Gugasian showed a scope of character qualities that added to his prosperity as a genius. He showed knowledge, genius, and unfaltering assurance. His daringness was clear in his capacity to design and execute a progression of bold bank heists, frequently late on a Friday night when security faculty were diminished.

Criminal Vocation:

Gugasian had no crook record prior to leaving on his bold heist binge. His law-breaker vocation was set apart by a line of high-profile bank thefts. His boldness was shown through his capacity to outmaneuver security frameworks, incapacitate cautions, and departure without abandoning any hint of his personality. He utilized different masks and redirection strategies to befuddle observers and agents.

The inspirations, characters, and criminal vocations of these famous heist geniuses offer an interesting look into the mind boggling factors that drive people and criminal associations to organize bold heists. Whether driven by monetary profit, aspiration, or a craving for acknowledgment, these brains feature the persevering through charm of fortune heists and the unfaltering assurance of the individuals who pick an existence of dauntlessness and wrongdoing. Their daring adventures challenge the best person-alities in policing security, making a permanent imprint on the universe of wrong-doing and interest.

Chapter 3

Treasures at Stake

The universe of fortune heists is a domain where the charm of unfathomable wealth meets with the daringness of criminal geniuses. These venturesome criminals put their focus on a portion of the world's most significant fortunes, be they inestimable works of art, uncommon gems, or notable curios. Their inspirations differ, yet the ongoing idea is a resolute craving for abundance that drives them to coordinate fastidiously arranged and trying heists. In this investigation, we dive into the fortunes in question, the objectives of these nervy endeavors, and the getting through interest that encompasses them.

The Appeal of Fortunes

The appeal of fortunes rises above time, spot, and culture. For centuries, mankind has been charmed by the gleam of gold, the radiance of gems, and the excellence of craftsmanship. Treasures address material abundance as well as verifiable and social importance, pervading them with a one of a kind charm that draws the two gatherers and crooks the same.

Authentic Importance: Many fortunes are significant for their material worth as well as for their verifiable significance. They act as substantial connections to the past, protecting the narratives and traditions of human advancements, craftsmen, and occasions. The charm of having a piece of history is a strong inspiration for gatherers and, tragically, for the individuals who look to take these curios.

Social Legacy: Fortunes frequently address a country's or a group's social legacy. From antiquated models to strict relics, these articles hold significant importance and are viewed as images of character. Securing and saving these social fortunes involves public pride and authentic congruity.

Imaginative Magnificence: A few fortunes are esteemed basically for their creative excellence. Whether it's a magnum opus by an eminent painter or a finely created piece of gems, the tasteful allure of these things rises above their monetary worth. Authorities are attracted to these items as benefactors of craftsmanship and excellence.

Financial Worth: obviously, the most prompt appeal of fortunes is their money related esteem. The commitment of untold abundance rouses criminal brains as well as entrepreneurial hoodlums who see the potential for a life changing bonus in the burglary of a significant craftsmanship or gem.

High-Profile Targets

The nervy hoodlums who focus on these fortunes are attracted to high-profile targets — spots and establishments where the world's most important and socially critical fortunes are housed. Exhibition halls, displays, banks, and, surprisingly, confidential assortments become the central places of daring heists. The high-profile nature of these objectives adds an additional layer of charm to the heists, as they catch the public's creative mind and the consideration of policing.

Exhibition halls and Displays: Galleries are much of the time gold mines of craftsmanship and verifiable relics. The possibility of taking inestimable canvases, figures, or uncommon relics is a convincing inspiration for nervy criminals. These organizations are likewise known for their strong safety efforts, making fruitful heists even more great.

Banks and Vaults: Banks are archives of monetary fortunes, yet they additionally house wellbeing store boxes that might contain important gems, records, or legacies. Criminal brains with information on security frameworks are attracted to these establishments, arranging trying heists that include breaking profoundly secure vaults.

Confidential Assortments: Well off people and gatherers frequently hoard private assortments of workmanship, gems, and verifiable antiquities. The appeal of focusing on these assortments lies in the potential for taking uncommon and important things that are less inclined to be safeguarded by broad safety efforts. In any case, the test is accessing these all around monitored homes.

Houses of God and Strict Destinations: Strict relics and curios can hold colossal social and verifiable importance. Church buildings and strict destinations house fortunes like cups, strict craftsmanship, and verifiable texts. While these spots might have profound worth, they are likewise viewed as focuses by venturesome cheats driven by the expected monetary profit.

Persevering through Interest

The persevering through interest with treasure heists originates from a blend of variables that enamor the public's creative mind and the media's consideration. These elements add to the persevering through appeal of fortune heists, making them the stuff of legends and legend.

Dauntlessness and Interest: The boldness of heists, the fastidious arranging included, and the capacity to outmaneuver imposing security frameworks make a quality of interest and secret. Venturesome criminals frequently utilize shrewd methodologies, masks, and redirection strategies, adding to the interest encompassing these endeavors.

Genuine Thrill rides: Fortune heists frequently look like the plotlines of exciting heist films. The general population is attracted to the genuine show, tension, and turns that work out in nervy heists. The way that these situation develop in reality, as opposed to on a film screen, makes them all the seriously spellbinding.

Criminal Geniuses: The baffling figures behind these bold heists become awesome characters. Their knowledge, creativity, and capacity to avoid policing the best personalities in security and examination. The public's interest with these lawbreaker brains is both a consequence of their dauntlessness and their capacity to stay on the loose for broadened periods.

Media Inclusion: The media assumes a vital part in enhancing the charm of fortune heists. Broad inclusion, including news reports, narratives, and element films, adds to the getting through interest with these adventures. Media consideration keeps these heists in the public eye long after they happen.

High Stakes and Outcomes: The high stakes of fortune heists, both as far as the possible monetary profit and the legitimate results of getting found out, add an additional layer of fervor. The prospect of crooks gambling with everything for a shot at unfathomable wealth is an exhilarating story.

Social and Verifiable Importance: Fortunes, whether they are workmanship, authentic antiques, or gems, are frequently attached to accounts of social and verifiable importance. The charm of fortunes is increased by the information that these things address a substantial connection to the past, interfacing us to individuals and occasions that formed our reality.

The immortal charm of fortunes in question, high-profile targets, and the getting through interest with daring heists meet up to make a dazzling universe of wrongdoing and interest. Daring cheats, driven by a scope of inspirations, challenge security frameworks, policing, public creative mind. The persevering through allure of these fortune heists lies in the appeal of abundance as well as in the tales, show, and awesome figures who populate this captivating and risky domain.

3.1 The historical and cultural significance of the stolen treasures

Taken treasures, whether they are extremely valuable craftsmanships, verifiable relics, or intriguing gems, hold a significant authentic and social importance. These fortunes are not just objects of material worth; they are storehouses of history, imaginativeness, and social character. At the point when bold cheats target and take such fortunes, they upset the verifiable continuum and social legacy, igniting shock and causing to notice the more extensive ramifications of their wrongdoings. In this investigation, we dive into the verifiable and social meaning of taken treasures, understanding the reason why their robbery is a blow not exclusively to their legitimate owners yet to mankind's aggregate legacy.

Saving History

Loves frequently act as unmistakable connections to the past, saving the set of experiences, stories, and traditions of human advancements, craftsmen, and occasions.

They give a window into former times, permitting us to interface with individuals and societies that preceded us.

Authentic Antiques: Many taken treasures incorporate verifiable antiquities like antiquated models, original copies, and relics. These articles offer experiences into the regular routines, convictions, and accomplishments of our predecessors. At the point when these curios are taken, the verifiable setting they give is lost.

Social Curios: Social relics envelop a great many items that hold social importance, from customary dress to strict images. These relics are fundamental for figuring out the social practices, customs, and conviction frameworks of various social orders. At the point when taken, the social information they convey is upset.

Authentic Archives: Taken verifiable reports, like uncommon compositions or letters, frequently shed light on significant authentic figures and occasions. They are essential hotspots for history specialists and researchers, empowering them to precisely remake the past.

Social Personality

Treasures are not simply protests; they are images of social personality and authentic coherence. They address the aggregate memory and shared upsides of a country or a group, and the robbery of these social images is an attack on that personality.

Public Pride: Fortunes held inside a country's lines are a wellspring of public pride. They act as images of a country's social accomplishments and verifiable heritage. The robbery of such fortunes is viewed as an attack against the country's personality.

Social Legacy: Many fortunes are important for a country's social legacy. These incorporate craftsmanships, strict relics, and curios that encapsulate the practices, customs, and history of a general public. Taken social legacy disturbs the congruity of these practices.

Verifiable Stories: Fortunes frequently assume a significant part in forming authentic stories. They give proof of significant occasions, social trades, and creative accomplishments. The burglary of such things can mutilate or eradicate segments of history.

Imaginative Magnificence

Notwithstanding their verifiable and social importance, a few fortunes are esteemed fundamentally for their creative excellence. The tasteful allure of these things rises above their monetary worth, making them a fundamental region of the planet creative and social legacy.

Show-stoppers of Workmanship: Canvases, figures, and different craftsmanships that have accomplished the situation with magnum opuses are loved for their creative brightness. The burglary of these works denies the universe of their tasteful and social worth.

Gems and Brightening Expressions: Valuable adornments, fine china, and enlivening workmanship pieces are respected for their craftsmanship and excellence. The robbery of these things denies the universe of their creative commitments.

Engineering Marvels: Fortunes may likewise incorporate structural miracles, like memorable structures, royal residences, or old landmarks. These designs are valued for their compositional excellence and social importance. When designated by criminals, they face the gamble of irreversible harm or annihilation.

Loss of Social Information

The robbery of fortunes reaches out past the quick material misfortune. It frequently brings about the deficiency of social information, customs, and verifiable setting that these articles give.

Social Practices: Fortunes frequently exemplify social practices and customs. For instance, a taken strict artifact might be an image of love or a social practice that conveys profound importance. At the point when taken, that social information is upset.

Verifiable Setting: Taken treasures give authentic setting to the antiquities and reports that encompass them. At the point when these articles are eliminated from their unique settings, the verifiable setting is lost, making it trying to figure out their full importance.

Social Trade: Many fortunes are the consequence of social trade and diverse associations. At the point when taken, the account of these trades and the subsequent combination of societies is divided.

Common Memory

Networks, whether they are strict, ethnic, or imaginative, frequently have an aggregate memory attached to specific fortunes. The burglary of these fortunes isn't just a misfortune for the local area yet additionally a deletion of their common history and personality.

Strict People group: Strict curios and relics hold profound importance for strict networks. At the point when taken, these networks lose a piece of their profound legacy.

Ethnic Character: Fortunes can likewise be images of ethnic personality, addressing the novel history and customs of explicit ethnic gatherings. The robbery of such fortunes upsets the story of these networks.

Imaginative Heritages: In the realm of workmanship, loves frequently act as foundations of creative inheritances. For example, the robbery of a renowned canvas disturbs the imaginative genealogy to which it has a place.

Global Strategy

Many fortunes have global importance, and their robbery can strain conciliatory relations between nations. Taken workmanship and antiques frequently become subjects of exchange and debates, including complex lawful and moral contemplations.

Bringing home: When fortunes are taken from one nation and end up in another, bringing home turns into a petulant issue. Nations might request the arrival of taken things, and exchanges can include numerous lawful and discretionary layers.

Global Agreements: Peaceful accords and accords have been laid out to address the bringing home of taken social ancient rarities. These arrangements give a lawful system to the arrival of taken fortunes to their original owners.

Plundering and Struggle: Fortunes that are taken during clashes or wars can have broad results. The plundering of social legacy frequently compounds political pressures and expands the social and verifiable harm brought about by the contention.

The Taken Fortunes That Resound

Certain taken fortunes have accomplished a degree of reputation and public acknowledgment that goes past their material or creative worth. These things become images of more extensive issues, like plundering, bringing home, and the security of social legacy.

Elgin Marbles: The Elgin Marbles, otherwise called the Parthenon Marbles, are an assortment of old style Greek marble models. They were eliminated from the Parthenon in Athens in the mid nineteenth 100 years by Ruler Elgin and later obtained by the English Gallery. Their expulsion has been a wellspring of debate, with Greece requesting their bringing home.

Rosetta Stone: The Rosetta Stone, which assumed an essential part in unraveling Egyptian pictographs, is currently housed in the English Exhibition hall. Egypt has long looked for the arrival of the stone as an image of its social legacy.

Nefertiti Bust: The Nefertiti Bust, a choice illustration of old Egyptian craftsmanship, is right now in Berlin's Neues Gallery. Egypt has looked for the arrival of the bust, which stays an intense image of the bringing home development.

Landmarks Men: The Landmarks Men were a gathering of people who worked during The Second Great War to recuperate and shield workmanship and social fortunes from robbery and harm. Their endeavors were memorialized in a book and a resulting film, carrying the issue of craftsmanship robbery to the public's consideration.

The Getting through Call for Bringing home

The burglary of fortunes is much of the time followed by a chorale of voices calling for bringing home. Nations, people group, and social gatherings request the arrival of taken things to their original owners, contending that these fortunes are a fundamental piece of their legacy.

Bringing home Developments: Bringing home developments have picked up speed as of late, with nations and organizations confronting expanding strain to return taken social antiques and fine arts. These developments are driven by a craving to right verifiable wrongs and reestablish social heritages.

Moral Contemplations: whether or not fortunes ought to be gotten back to their places of beginning involves moral discussion. Contentions for bringing home frequently spin around correcting verifiable treacheries and tending to the moral elements of taken treasures.

Lawful Systems: Worldwide legitimate structures and arrangements, for example, the 1970 UNESCO Show on the Method for Disallowing and Forestalling the Unlawful Import, Commodity, and Move of Responsibility for Property, give direction on the bringing home of taken social relics.

Safeguarding Social Legacy

Endeavors to safeguard social legacy and forestall the burglary of fortunes have turned into a worldwide need. Exhibition halls, displays, and state run administrations have executed measures to protect social curios and works of art from daring criminals.

Upgraded Security: Exhibition halls and organizations lodging important fortunes have put resources into improved security frameworks, including observation, cautions, and access control. These actions are intended to hinder hoodlums and safeguard the fortunes.

Provenance Exploration: Provenance research, which looks to lay out the historical backdrop of responsibility for work of art or curio, has turned into a critical device in recognizing taken treasures. By following a thing's set of experiences, specialists can decide if it was gained through unlawful means.

Public Mindfulness: Raising public mindfulness about the issue of taken social curios and the moral contemplations encompassing their securing and proprietorship has turned into a vital piece of endeavors to safeguard social legacy.

3.2 The beauty and value of the art, artifacts, and wealth

Workmanship, relics, and abundance have enthralled human creative mind for quite a long time, rising above societies, periods, and topographies. They address a different exhibit of human accomplishments, from the ethereal magnificence of a Renaissance painting to the unpredictable craftsmanship of a verifiable relic to the material wealth of huge fortunes. In this investigation, we dive into the significant magnificence and worth that these fortunes typify, understanding the manners by which they shape the world, impact people, and make a permanent imprint on our shared mindset.

Craftsmanship: Stylish Tastefulness and Social Importance

Craftsmanship has been a lasting wellspring of motivation and interest for humankind. It envelops a large number of innovative articulations, from painting and model to writing, music, and performing expressions. The magnificence and worth of workmanship are complex, as it serves both tasteful and social jobs.

Stylish Magnificence:

Stylish magnificence is at the center of craftsmanship's worth. The brush strokes of an expert painter, the amicable songs of a writer, or the many-sided plan of a model summon feelings, wonderment, and reverence. Workmanship offers a visual, hear-able, and tangible experience that rises above words and discusses straightforwardly with the human spirit.

Social Importance:

Workmanship likewise conveys significant social importance. It is an impression of a general public's qualities, convictions, and verifiable setting. Workmanship gives a window into the past, offering experiences into the customs, methods of reasoning, and inventive soul of a specific general setting. The worth of workmanship, in this specific circumstance, stretches out past its stylish allure and envelops its job as a social time container.

Verifiable and Contemporary Workmanship:

The worth of workmanship traverses verifiable and contemporary articulations. While verifiable craftsmanship offers an association with the past and a comprehension of the development of creative structures, contemporary workmanship challenges assumptions and mirrors the dynamism of current society. The magnificence in verifiable workmanship lies in its immortal allure, while contemporary craftsmanship frequently looks to incite thought and question existing standards.

Social Ancient rarities: Gatekeepers of History and Character

Ancient rarities address unmistakable remainders of our past. These articles, frequently with social, authentic, or archeological importance, are gold mines of information and understanding into old developments, human accomplishments, and verifiable accounts.

Safeguarding of History:

Antiquities, whether old instruments, earthenware, or strict relics, save history. They act as actual records of a general public's lifestyle, mechanical headways, and social practices. These articles give the lacking parts to the riddle of mankind's set of experiences.

Social Personality:

Ancient rarities are significant of social personality. They frequently exemplify the practices, customs, and conviction frameworks of a specific gathering or progress. Antiquities are not simply protests; they are images of character, and the excellence in this lies an option for them to join individuals across ages and geographic limits.

Archeological Revelations:

Archeological unearthings keep on uncovering stowed away fortunes and revealed insight into old developments. The revelation of very much protected relics, whether in submerged wrecks or old entombment locales, reveals an abundance of verifiable and social data.

Unmistakable Abundance: Past the Material

The idea of abundance stretches out past the gathering of material resources; it includes a more extensive range of overflow, impact, and heritage. The magnificence and worth of abundance lie in the capacity to mold lives, support causes, and make an enduring imprint on society.

Monetary Thriving:

Monetary abundance is maybe the most traditional comprehension of riches. It addresses the collection of resources, cash, and monetary assets. The magnificence in monetary abundance is the opportunity and opportunity it offers to people and the ability to change survives magnanimity and business venture.

Scholarly Riches:

Scholarly abundance includes information, mastery, and thoughts. The worth of scholarly abundance is an option for its to drive development, imagination, and progress. Scholarly abundance encourages instruction, research, and the quest for new skylines.

Social Riches:

Social abundance relates to the safeguarding of social legacy, creative articulations, and customs. Social abundance is the manager of authentic accounts, masterfulness, and aggregate memory. It improves social orders and highlights the significance of legacy.

Natural Riches:

Ecological abundance connects with the wellbeing of our planet, including the wealth of normal assets and the conservation of biological systems. The magnificence in ecological abundance is its part in supporting life and protecting the regular world for people in the future.

Human Resources:

Human resources addresses the abilities, gifts, and capability of people. The worth of human resources is found in the limit of individuals to add to society, whether through their work, advancement, or commitments to their networks.

Moral and Moral Abundance:

Moral and moral abundance allude to the standards, values, and moral norms that guide people and social orders. The excellence in moral and moral abundance is the ability to encourage moral way of behaving, social attachment, and the benefit of all.

The Magnificence of Ownership: From Workmanship Gatherers to Fortune Developers

The magnificence of having craftsmanship, ancient rarities, and abundance isn't restricted to the characteristic worth of these resources. It stretches out to the encounters, obligations, and honors that accompany such possession.

Craftsmanship Gatherers:

Craftsmanship gatherers, whether people or foundations, experience the excellence of workmanship on a significant level. They have the honor of being stewards of imaginative excellence, protecting it for people in the future and imparting it to the world. Workmanship authorities frequently become benefactors of specialists, supporting the making of new magnificence.

Craftsmanship Keepers:

Craftsmanship keepers are the overseers of imaginative excellence, liable for organizing and saving assortments. Their job stretches out to the curation of displays and the production of accounts that guide guests through the universe of workmanship. The magnificence in this job is the capacity to shape the public's insight of craftsmanship.

Abundance Manufacturers:

The individuals who gather abundance through monetary, scholarly, or social means become draftsmen of their own predetermination. They have the ability to set out open doors, support causes, and leave enduring inheritances. The excellence in creating financial stability is the capacity to mold one's life and the existences of others.

Generosity: Sharing Overflow

The magnificence of abundance is amplified when making positive change is utilized. Magnanimity, the demonstration of giving, addresses the convergence of riches and a longing to better the world. It significantly affects society and offers a brief look into the excellence of shared overflow.

Schooling and Exploration:

Magnanimous endeavors in training and exploration add to the progression of information, development, and the advancement of society. Establishments and people frequently store grants, research awards, and instructive projects to sustain scholarly riches.

Social Conservation:

Magnanimity likewise assumes a pivotal part in social safeguarding. Financing exhibition halls, authentic destinations, and imaginative undertakings guarantees that social abundance is passed down to people in the future. The magnificence of social safeguarding lies in the propagation of legacy.

Social Government assistance and Helpful Goals:

Charity resolves social issues and helpful purposes, going from neediness lightening to medical care arrangement. The excellence of magnanimous endeavors here is the ability to change lives, elevate networks, and proposition trust and poise to those out of luck.

The Workmanship Market: A Universe of Speculation and Energy

The craftsmanship market fills in as a novel crossing point of workmanship, riches, and venture. It encapsulates the duality of workmanship as both a stylish fortune and a monetary resource.

Speculation Worth:

Workmanship, especially pieces by famous craftsmen, frequently values in esteem over the long run. For gatherers, this double excellence as a stylish show-stopper and a monetary venture is a main thrust in the craftsmanship market. The appeal of gathering lies in the potential for critical profits from speculation.

Enthusiasm for Craftsmanship:

Numerous workmanship gatherers are driven by a profound energy for craftsmanship. They value the magnificence of workmanship in the entirety of its structures, from traditional to contemporary, and partake in the close to home association that craftsmanship brings to their lives. Their affection for craftsmanship rises above its monetary worth.

Workmanship Displays and Closeout Houses:

Craftsmanship exhibitions and sale houses are central members in the workmanship market. They work with the trading of craftsmanship, and their aptitude and curation frequently guide gatherers in their quest for excellence and worth. The magnificence in this part of the craftsmanship world is the capacity to associate gatherers with extraordinary bits of workmanship.

Difficulties and Contentions: The Double Idea of Workmanship and Riches

The interchange of workmanship and abundance isn't without its difficulties and debates. These emerge from the strain between workmanship as a social fortune and a monetary resource.

Social Conservation versus Confidential Possession:

One of the focal contentions in the craftsmanship world is the pressure between the social protection of workmanship and its confidential possession. The excellence of craftsmanship as a social fortune is some of the time in conflict with its status as a ware.

Provenance and Possession Cases:

Craftsmanships with questioned possession chronicles frequently flash fights in court and contentions. Questions encompassing the actual owners of works of art, especially those that were lost or taken during seasons of contention, can raise moral, legitimate, and authentic worries.

Evaluating and Theory:

The workmanship market is frequently described by estimating unpredictability and hypothesis. Speculative purchasing can prompt swelled costs and market bubbles, which can bring about monetary misfortunes for financial backers and bring up issues about the morals of benefitting from workmanship.

Bringing home and Compensation:

The bringing home of taken or socially huge craftsmanships is a perplexing issue that crosses with inquiries of possession and social conservation. Requires the bringing home of fine arts to their nations of beginning highlight the moral and verifiable elements of workmanship proprietorship.

Inheritance and Life span: Saving Magnificence for What's in store

Protecting the excellence and worth of craftsmanship, relics, and abundance for people in the future is a significant obligation. It requires cautious stewardship, moral contemplations, and an acknowledgment of the job these fortunes play in forming the world.

Workmanship Preservation:

Workmanship preservation is the act of saving the actual honesty of craftsmanship and ancient rarities. It guarantees that the excellence of these articles perseveres over the long haul, permitting people in the future to see the value in them as they were expected.

Gallery Stewardship:

Exhibition halls assume a fundamental part in safeguarding workmanship and social curios for people in the future. They go about as stewards of social abundance, protecting craftsmanship from disintegration and making it available to general society.

Generous Undertakings:

Magnanimous endeavors, including the foundation of establishments and trusts, effectively guarantee that the magnificence of social fortunes is kept up with and that their worth keeps on helping society.

Instruction and Effort:

Instruction and effort endeavors present the magnificence of workmanship and social importance to people in the future. These endeavors plan to motivate an appreciation for workmanship and curios and an acknowledgment of their part in molding mankind's set of experiences.

Moral Proprietorship:

Moral proprietorship includes straightforward provenance, mindful stewardship, and adherence to legitimate and moral rules in the obtaining and offer of workmanship and antiquities. Moral proprietorship guarantees that the magnificence and worth of these articles are saved with trustworthiness.

Excellence and Worth Divulged

The excellence and worth of workmanship, relics, and abundance are diverse and significant. They reverberate in their natural characteristics as well as in their capacity to shape human encounters, protect social legacy, and leave heritages that persevere through the ages. Craftsmanship and curios offer a window into our aggregate past, giving verifiable setting and social importance. Riches, whether monetary, scholarly, or social, fills in as a vessel for a potential open door, progress, and charity. The crossing point of workmanship and riches, as found in the craftsmanship market, highlights the double idea of magnificence as a stylish fortune and a monetary resource. While difficulties and contentions exist, the obligation of saving excellence and an incentive for people in the future remaining parts an immortal and fundamental undertaking. In grasping the significant excellence and worth of workmanship, antiquities, and abundance, we recognize their persevering through importance in molding the world and the heritage they leave for the people who follow.

Chapter 4

The Great Heists

The Incomparable Heists have consistently held an interest for both the criminal hidden world and policing the same. These trying demonstrations of burglary, interest, and high-stakes show have caught the public's creative mind for a really long time. From the nervy capers of the Wild West to the refined cybercrimes of the cutting edge age, the universe of heists is a rich embroidery of shrewd crooks, wonderful preparation, and the tenacious quest for equity.

Perhaps of the earliest heist on record traces all the way back to the seventeenth 100 years in London, Britain. In 1671, the striking and shrewd hoodlum William Davis executed a wonderful burglary at the Pinnacle of London. This brassy trick is accepted to be perhaps the earliest kept heist ever, making way for century of criminal advancement.

As time elapsed, heists advanced close by innovation and cultural changes. In the nineteenth 100 years, the American Wild West turned into a hotbed of thinking for even a moment to prepare and bank burglaries. Figures like Jesse James and Butch Cassidy acquired reputation for their bold endeavors, burglarizing banks and sidestepping lawmen across the boondocks. These awesome criminals became legends by their own doing, sustaining the mythos of the incredible heist.

The twentieth century carried with it another period of heists, portrayed by refinement and accuracy. In 1971, a gathering of cheats executed a staggering heist at the Lloyds Bank in London, an accomplishment that would stand out forever as the "Pastry specialist Road Burglary." The criminals burrowed their direction into the bank's vault, snatching a mind blowing take of over £3 million (comparable to almost £40 million today). The Pastry specialist Road Burglary denoted a defining moment in the realm of heists, exhibiting a degree of arranging and execution that was extraordinary.

The universe of heists proceeded to advance, and the 21st century brought new difficulties and open doors for lawbreakers. As innovation progressed, so did the strategies utilized by hoodlums. Cybercrime turned into a central part in the realm of heists, with programmers focusing on banks, enterprises, and even legislatures. The heists of the computerized age were less about weapons and veils and more about lines of code and complex calculations.

One of the most notorious digital heists happened in 2016 when programmers designated the Bangladesh Bank. They figured out how to penetrate the bank's frameworks and endeavored to take almost a billion bucks. While not the cash was all effectively moved, the heist actually positions as quite possibly of the biggest cybercrime ever. The refinement and daringness of such demonstrations have made them a focal concentration for policing and network protection specialists all over the planet.

The charm of heists reaches out past the criminal viewpoint. Hollywood has embraced the class with great affection, delivering endless movies that romanticize and perform these trying accomplishments. Notable heist films like "Sea's Eleven," "Intensity," and "The Italian Work" have become works of art, engaging crowds and propagating the fantasy of the cleverness and charming cheat.

However, the truth of heists is not even close to exciting. It frequently includes savagery, treachery, and the consistent anxiety toward being caught. For each effective heist, there are incalculable others that end in a fiasco. The dangers are high, and the prizes, while possibly worthwhile, frequently come at a precarious cost.

The intentions behind heists fluctuate broadly. A few hoodlums are driven by monetary benefit, while others look for retribution or political goals. The sheer dauntlessness of these demonstrations, no matter what the inspiration, has kept on dazzling the public's creative mind.

From the beginning of time, the quest for equity has been a consistent subject in the realm of heists. Policing have enthusiastically sought after the culprits of these wrongdoings, frequently depending on shrewd investigators and state of the art innovation to find the crooks. The strain between the lawbreaker and the criminal investigator, the hoodlum and the follower, has been a characterizing component of heist stories.

Perhaps of the most unbelievable analyst chasing heisters was Forthcoming Serpico. His work during the 1960s and 1970s as a New York City cop, principally in the casually dressed division, was instrumental in battling coordinated wrongdoing and checking debasement inside the police force. He put his life in extreme danger to uncover debasement inside the division and made light of a vital job in taking famous hoodlums.

Serpico's story was subsequently deified in the 1973 film "Serpico," which featured Al Pacino in the lead spot. The film exhibited the risks and difficulties looked by the people who try to deal with heisters, featuring the ethical issues and individual penances associated with such pursuits.

The wait-and-see game between policing heisters has just become more perplexing with time. Lawbreakers have embraced progressively modern strategies, utilizing innovation for their potential benefit and remaining one stride in front of the specialists.

The cutting edge investigator should be well informed and versatile, confronting a dynamic and steadily developing scene of crime.

As of late, the peculiarity of heists has reached out past conventional crook undertakings. Workmanship heists, specifically, have caught the public's creative mind. The robbery of precious compositions and social relics has turned into a main issue for exhibition halls and displays around the world. These high-profile burglaries frequently include perplexing preparation and, at times, crafted by profoundly gifted cheats.

The robbery of Edvard Chomp's notable painting "The Shout" in 2004 was one such high-profile workmanship heist. The cheats broke into the Chomp Exhibition hall in Oslo, Norway, and grabbed the well known work of art, esteemed at more than $100 million. The heist sent shockwaves through the workmanship world, and the composition was ultimately recuperated in 2006.

The heist of "The Shout" highlights the worth put on social legacy and the lengths to which hoodlums will go to benefit from it. It likewise features the significance of global collaboration in finding taken craftsmanship, as the work of art was eventually tracked down in the possession of a crook network in Norway.

Notwithstanding workmanship heists, one more arising pattern in the realm of heists includes the burglary of digital currency. With the ascent of advanced monetary standards like Bitcoin, hoodlums have tracked down new open doors for robbery. Hacking into cryptographic money trades and wallets has turned into a rewarding undertaking, with programmers grabbing a huge number of dollars in virtual cash.

The 2014 heist of Mt. Gox, when one of the biggest Bitcoin trades, remains as a critical illustration of this new boondocks in crime. The trade declared financial insolvency in the wake of losing around 850,000 Bitcoins, many inquiries actually encompass the personality of the programmers dependable.

The heist of cryptographic money raises exceptional difficulties for policing, the advanced idea of these resources frequently makes it hard to follow and recuperate taken reserves. It likewise features the requirement for improved network safety measures to safeguard the developing interest in computerized monetary standards.

While heists have been romanticized in film and writing, recalling the genuine outcomes of these lawbreaker acts is significant. Heists can prompt viciousness, injury for casualties, and the disturbance of lives and occupations. Policing and security specialists constantly work to forestall heists and deal with those mindful.

In spite of the dangers and results, the charm of the extraordinary heist perseveres. It is a demonstration of the human interest with boldness, shrewd, and the excitement of the pursuit. The heist classification keeps on advancing, mirroring the changing scene of wrongdoing and innovation. The narratives of heists, both genuine and fictitious, will probably keep on charming our creative mind for a long time into the future.

4.1 A series of chapters, each dedicated to a famous heist

The universe of wrongdoing and interest is packed with accounts of trying heists that have charmed the creative mind of people in general and left policing in amazement of the boldness and clever of the culprits. Every one of these well known heists, with its one of a kind conditions and characters, has its own place ever. In the accompanying series of parts, we dive into the subtleties of the absolute most renowned heists at any point committed, traversing various periods and areas.

The Incomparable Train Burglary (1963)

In 1963, a gathering of trying hoodlums executed what might become perhaps of the most popular heist ever: The Incomparable Train Burglary. Everything started when a posse of 15 men, drove by the brains Bruce Reynolds, devised a strategy to ransack a Regal Mail train going from Glasgow to London. The train was conveying a significant measure of money, including banknotes and coins.

The pack fastidiously ready for the heist, learning the train's timetable and courses, and cautiously choosing a distant area referred to as Bridego Extension as the best spot to trap the train. The evening of August 8, 1963, the pack got a move on. They messed with the railroad signals, stopping the train, and afterward continued to overwhelm the train's team and safety crew.

With a solid feeling of accuracy and proficiency, they moved the packs of money from the train into holding up vehicles. The posse grabbed an astounding take of £2.6 million, which is comparable to over £50 million today. This nervy burglary stood out as truly newsworthy overall and transformed the pack into moment legends.

The outcome of The Incomparable Train Burglary was, to some extent, because of the fastidious preparation and execution of the heist, yet it at last prompted the destruction of many involved. A tremendous manhunt was sent off, and throughout the long term, the majority of the gangsters were captured and dealt with. In spite of their underlying achievement, a considerable lot of them carried out lengthy jail punishments.

The Isabella Stewart Gardner Gallery Heist (1990)

In 1990, one of the most well known craftsmanship heists in history occurred at the Isabella Stewart Gardner Exhibition hall in Boston, Massachusetts. Two cheats camouflaged as cops acquired section to the historical center in the early long periods of Walk 18, 1990. They continued to incapacitate the safety officers and completed a carefully arranged craftsmanship heist.

The criminals snatched 13 significant bits of craftsmanship, including works by Vermeer, Degas, and Rembrandt. The complete worth of the taken workmanship was assessed to be around $500 million, making it one of the biggest craftsmanship heists at any point recorded. The robbery sent shockwaves through the workmanship world and set off an overall chase after the taken magnum opuses.

Notwithstanding broad examinations and a $10 million prize for data prompting the recuperation of the taken craftsmanship, the compositions stay missing right up to the present day. The Isabella Stewart Gardner Historical center heist remains as a demonstration of the daringness of craftsmanship cheats and the getting through secret of perplexing wrongdoings.

The Banco Focal Robbery (2005)

In August 2005, a gathering of hoodlums in Fortaleza, Brazil, executed an exceptional heist that left specialists dumbfounded. The objective was the Banco Focal, the national bank of Brazil, and the hoodlums utilized a daring strategy to get close enough to the vault.

The lawbreakers leased a business property in the city and started digging a passage that drove straightforwardly under the bank. The passage, which was masterfully built and very much ventilated, extended for north of 78 meters, furnishing the hoodlums with an incognito section point.

When inside the bank's vault, the criminals figured out how to incapacitate the security frameworks and grabbed roughly 160 million Brazilian reais, comparable to around $70 million. The heist was found just two days some other time when the bank's representatives showed up for work and understood the cash was absent.

Notwithstanding a broad manhunt and examinations, the majority of the hoodlums engaged with the Banco Focal Thievery figured out how to dodge catch. The daringness and refinement of this heist made it one of the most popular and confounding in ongoing history.

The Antwerp Jewel Heist (2003)

Antwerp, Belgium, is known as the jewel capital of the world, and in 2003, a gathering of Italian criminals executed one of the most brassy precious stone heists at any point recorded. The objective was the Antwerp Jewel Center, which housed a colossal measure of jewels, gold, and other valuable pearls.

The hoodlums figured out how to get close enough to the profoundly gotten vault by impairing the intricate security framework. Over a long end of the week in February, the lawbreakers worked methodicallly, penetrating through various layers of safety, including the vault entryway itself. They snatched an astounding take of jewels, gold, and other valuable things worth an expected $100 million.

Notwithstanding their underlying achievement, the cheats abandoned important signs, and examiners had the option to follow them to a lawbreaker network in Italy. A large number of those engaged with the heist were captured and dealt with, however a significant part of the taken jewels stays missing right up 'til now.

The Hatton Nursery Heist (2015)

In April 2015, a gathering of older hoodlums executed a heist that blew some minds and caught the creative mind of the general population. The Hatton Nursery Safe Store Organization, situated in London's well known adornments locale, was the objective of their brassy arrangement.

The group, which became known as the "Awful Granddads" because of their old age, utilized their experience to design and execute the heist cautiously. They acquired passage to the structure by boring through a two-meter-thick substantial wall, permitting them admittance to the vault's items.

Over the Easter weekend, the pack exhausted the store boxes of money, adornments, and different resources. The specific worth of the taken products is assessed to be around £14 million.

While the underlying progress of the Hatton Nursery Heist astonished many, the pack's old age didn't keep them from falling under the examination of the law. After some time, the greater part of the gangsters were captured and dealt with, carrying out jail punishments for their daring wrongdoing.

The Banco Focal Thievery (2005)

In August 2005, a gathering of cheats in Fortaleza, Brazil, executed an unprecedented heist that left specialists dumbfounded. The objective was the Banco Focal, the national bank of Brazil, and the criminals utilized a daring strategy to get close enough to the vault.

The crooks leased a business property in the city and started digging a passage that drove straightforwardly under the bank. The passage, which was skillfully built and very much ventilated, extended for more than 78 meters, furnishing the hoodlums with a secretive section point.

When inside the bank's vault, the cheats figured out how to impair the security frameworks and snatched roughly 160 million Brazilian reais, comparable to around $70 million. The heist was found just two days some other time when the bank's representatives showed up for work and understood the cash was absent.

Regardless of a broad manhunt and examinations, the majority of the criminals associated with the Banco Focal Robbery figured out how to sidestep catch. The daringness and refinement of this heist made it one of the most well known and confounding in ongoing history.

The Isabella Stewart Gardner Exhibition hall Heist (1990)

In 1990, one of the most renowned craftsmanship heists in history occurred at the Isabella Stewart Gardner Exhibition hall in Boston, Massachusetts. Two hoodlums camouflaged as cops acquired passage to the exhibition hall in the early long stretches of Walk 18, 1990. They continued to incapacitate the safety officers and completed a fastidiously arranged craftsmanship heist.

The criminals snatched 13 important bits of workmanship, including works by Vermeer, Degas, and Rembrandt. The complete worth of the taken workmanship was assessed to be around $500 million, making it one of the biggest craftsmanship heists at any point recorded. The robbery sent shockwaves through the workmanship world and set off an overall chase after the taken magnum opuses.

In spite of broad examinations and a $10 million prize for data prompting the recuperation of the taken workmanship, the canvases stay missing right up 'til now. The Isabella Stewart Gardner Gallery heist remains as a demonstration of the daringness of workmanship criminals and the persevering through secret of perplexing wrongdoings.

The Antwerp Precious stone Heist (2003)

Antwerp, Belgium, is known as the precious stone capital of the world, and in 2003, a gathering of Italian cheats executed one of the most brassy jewel heists at any point recorded. The objective was the Antwerp Jewel Center, which housed a colossal measure of jewels, gold, and other valuable pearls.

The cheats figured out how to get to the profoundly gotten vault by impairing the complicated security framework. Over a long end of the week in February, the hoodlums worked efficiently, boring through various layers of safety, including the vault entryway itself. They grabbed a surprising take of jewels, gold, and other valuable things worth an expected $100 million.

Notwithstanding their underlying achievement, the hoodlums abandoned significant hints, and examiners had the option to follow them to a crook network in Italy. A considerable lot of those engaged with the heist were secured and dealt with, yet a significant piece of the taken jewels stays missing right up to the present day.

The Incomparable Train Burglary (1963)

In 1963, a gathering of trying hoodlums executed what might become perhaps of the most well known heist ever: The Incomparable Train Burglary. Everything started when a pack of 15 men, drove by the brains Bruce Reynolds, devised a strategy to burglarize an Imperial Mail train venturing out from Glasgow to London. The train was conveying a significant measure of money, including banknotes and coins.

The posse fastidiously ready for the heist, learning the train's timetable and courses, and cautiously choosing a distant area referred to as Bridego Extension as the best spot to snare the train. The evening of August 8, 1963, the group got a move on. They messed with the rail line signals, stopping the train, and afterward continued to overwhelm the train's group and safety faculty.

4.2 Detailed accounts of the planning, execution, and aftermath

The preparation, execution, and fallout of heists address an intricate interchange of technique, trying, and outcomes. From careful plotting to high-stakes activities and the steady quest for equity, these components meet up in entrancing ways in the realm of heists. In the accompanying nitty gritty records, we investigate the absolute most popular heists, uncovering the complex preparation, venturesome execution, and frequently emotional consequence of these exceptional lawbreaker tries.

The Incomparable Train Burglary (1963)

The preparation and execution of The Incomparable Train Burglary in 1963 stand as a demonstration of the daringness and fastidious arrangements of the posse drove by Bruce Reynolds. The heist was a considering endeavoring to burglarize a Regal Mail train heading out from Glasgow to London, known for conveying significant measures of money, including banknotes and coins. It was, undoubtedly, quite possibly of the most renowned heist ever.

The fastidious arranging started with the pack learning the train's timetable and courses, in the long run focusing in on a distant area referred to as Bridego Scaffold as the ideal spot for their heist. The site was picked for its isolated nature and distance from any police headquarters, guaranteeing that the posse had the advantage in the event of conflict.

The evening of August 8, 1963, was the picked second for the daring activity. The posse utilized their insight into the rail line framework and messed with the signs, making the train stop. With this redirection set up, they continued to overwhelm the train's group and safety crew.

The pack's execution was set apart by accuracy and proficiency. They quickly moved the packs of money from the train into holding up vehicles. In no time flat, the group snatched a stunning take of £2.6 million, comparable to over £50 million today. The boldness of The Incomparable Train Burglary stood out as truly newsworthy around the world, and the gangsters were moment legends, celebrated for their daring accomplishment.

Notwithstanding, the progress of the heist was at last its defeat. The tremendous manhunt that followed, driven by constant policing, prompted the fear of the greater part of the gangsters throughout the long term. Notwithstanding their underlying achievement, large numbers of them carried out lengthy jail punishments, and the nervy heist is recognized as one of the most renowned ever.

The Isabella Stewart Gardner Historical center Heist (1990)

The preparation and execution of the Isabella Stewart Gardner Historical center heist in 1990 were set apart by an elevated degree of complexity and dauntlessness. The objective was the Isabella Stewart Gardner Gallery in Boston, Massachusetts, eminent for its precious workmanship assortment. The evening of Walk 18, 1990, two hoodlums, masked as cops, acquired section to the gallery and executed a fastidiously arranged workmanship heist.

The heist was set apart by its dauntlessness, as the cheats incapacitated the safety officers and continued to exhaust the historical center's displays of valuable workmanship deliberately. Thirteen significant pieces, including works by Vermeer, Degas, and Rembrandt, were taken, with the absolute worth of the workmanship assessed at around $500 million.

The daring burglary sent shockwaves through the workmanship world, setting off an overall chase after the taken show-stoppers. In spite of broad examinations and a $10 million prize for data prompting the recuperation of the craftsmanship, the compositions stay missing right up 'til now.

The result of the Isabella Stewart Gardner Exhibition hall heist is a demonstration of the persevering through secret of perplexing violations. Notwithstanding endeavors by policing the craftsmanship local area, the taken workmanship keeps on escaping recuperation, leaving a void in the realm of workmanship and an enduring tradition of quite possibly of the most bold heist ever.

The Banco Focal Thievery (2005)

The preparation and execution of the Banco Focal Thievery in Fortaleza, Brazil, in August 2005, exhibited a degree of dauntlessness and fastidious arranging that left specialists surprised. The objective was the Banco Focal, the national bank of Brazil, lodging a huge amount of cash.

The lawbreakers leased a business property in the city, starting a mind boggling activity to dig a passage that drove straightforwardly under the bank. The passage, stretching out for north of 78 meters, was skillfully built and very much ventilated, furnishing the hoodlums with an undercover section highlight the bank's vault.

Inside the bank, the hoodlums figured out how to incapacitate the security frameworks with accuracy, grabbing roughly 160 million Brazilian reais, identical to around $70 million. The brassy idea of the heist was apparent in the way that it required two days for the bank's representatives to find the cash was absent upon their re-visitation of work.

Regardless of broad examinations and a cross country manhunt, the greater part of the criminals engaged with the Banco Focal Robbery figured out how to dodge catch. The dauntlessness and complexity of the heist made it one of the most renowned and baffling in late history. The criminals' trying execution and careful arrangements brought about a wrongdoing that tested policing to deal with them.

The Antwerp Precious stone Heist (2003)

The preparation and execution of the Antwerp Precious stone Heist in 2003 exhibited the daringness and careful methodology of the Italian cheats included. Antwerp, Belgium, is eminent as the jewel capital of the world, making it an ideal objective for lawbreakers looking for valuable diamonds.

The hoodlums accessed the exceptionally gotten Antwerp Jewel Center, home to an immense measure of jewels, gold, and other valuable things. What put this heist aside was the craftiness and assurance of the lawbreakers to cripple the mind boggling security framework.

Over a long end of the week in February, the criminals methodicallly bored through various layers of safety, including the vault entryway itself. The outcome was a stunning take of jewels, gold, and other valuable things assessed to be worth around $100 million.

Notwithstanding their underlying achievement, the hoodlums passed on important hints that permitted specialists to follow them to a lawbreaker network in Italy. A large number of those engaged with the heist were captured and dealt with. By the by, a critical piece of the taken pearls stays missing right up to the present day, a demonstration of the daringness and bold execution of the Antwerp Precious stone Heist.

The Hatton Nursery Heist (2015)

The preparation and execution of the Hatton Nursery Heist in 2015 were set apart by the unforeseen contribution of a gathering of older hoodlums, suitably nicknamed the "Terrible Granddads." The objective was the Hatton Nursery Safe Store Organization, arranged in London's prestigious gems region, making it an appealing objective for a gathering of experienced crooks.

The pack utilized their old age for their potential benefit, cautiously arranging and executing the heist. They acquired section to the structure by penetrating through a two-meter-thick substantial wall, furnishing them with admittance to the vault's items.

Over the Easter weekend, the pack exhausted the store boxes of money, gems, and different assets, hoarding an expected worth of £14 million in taken merchandise. The heist's underlying achievement surprised everyone, given the old age of the gangsters, yet it eventually prompted their catch.

Over the long haul, a large portion of the gangsters were caught and dealt with, carrying out jail punishments for their nervy wrongdoing. The Hatton Nursery Heist fills in as an update that age isn't really an obstruction with regards to the venturesome execution of criminal plans.

These point by point records of renowned heists outline the preparation, execution, and consequence of unprecedented lawbreaker tries. From The Incomparable Train Burglary's venturesome heist in 1963 to the getting through secret of the Isabella Stewart Gardner Exhibition hall heist, each heist features the dauntlessness, accuracy, and refinement of hoodlums looking for significant additions.

The Banco Focal Thievery in Brazil, the Antwerp Jewel Heist in Belgium, and the Hatton Nursery Heist in London are instances of bold heists that tested policing and transformed history. For each situation, the outcomes of these nervy activities differed, from sidestepping catch to getting through imprisonment.

The universe of heists is described by bold preparation, exact execution, and the determined quest for equity. These records act as a demonstration of the getting through charm of high-stakes burglaries and the interest of bold crooks, guaranteeing that the universe of heists will keep on enthralling our creative mind for a long time into the future.

4.3 Exploration of the stolen treasures and their impact

The taken fortunes from heists are something beyond actual resources; they are images of venturesome violations that lastingly affect the universes of workmanship, money, and culture. The narratives of these taken fortunes, and their ensuing investigation, act as a demonstration of the persevering through charm of heists and the many-sided trap of outcomes they leave afterward.

The Taken Fortunes of the Isabella Stewart Gardner Historical center Heist (1990)

The taken fortunes from the Isabella Stewart Gardner Historical center heist in 1990 have become amazing, for their characteristic worth as well as for the vast void they left in the realm of craftsmanship. The heist was fastidiously executed, with the cheats grabbing 13 extremely valuable bits of workmanship, including works by prestigious specialists like Vermeer, Degas, and Rembrandt. The complete assessed worth of the taken workmanship is around $500 million.

The effect of the taken fortunes from this heist is complex. As a matter of some importance, the workmanship world experienced a gigantic misfortune. The taken works of art were something beyond important; they were social fortunes. Their vanishing made a void throughout the entire existence of craftsmanship, leaving workmanship devotees and researchers grieving the deficiency of these show-stoppers. The taken workmanship stays a subject of interest and hypothesis, with many expecting their possible recuperation.

The monetary results of the Isabella Stewart Gardner Historical center heist were critical also. The taken fortunes, esteemed at a galactic aggregate, addressed a significant disaster for the craftsmanship market. Their burglary brought up issues about the security of craftsmanship organizations and the requirement for further developed measures to safeguard significant social ancient rarities.

The taken fortunes' effect stretched out past the universe of workmanship and money. The daringness and careful preparation of the heist left an enduring heritage in the chronicles of criminal history. The cheats, regardless of staying at large, became notable figures in the realm of wrongdoing, making a permanent imprint on the class of heists.

Notwithstanding broad examinations and a $10 million prize for data prompting the recuperation of the taken workmanship, the compositions stay missing. The unsettled status of the taken fortunes fills in as a steady sign of the persevering through secret of strange wrongdoings and the tradition of brassy heists.

The Puzzling Destiny of the Antwerp Precious stone Heist Fortunes (2003)

The taken fortunes from the Antwerp Jewel Heist in 2003, which incorporated a tremendous amount of precious stones, gold, and valuable things esteemed at around $100 million, remain covered in secret. The actual heist was set apart by its careful preparation and daring execution, bringing about an amazing take of significant products.

The effect of the taken fortunes from this heist reaches out a long ways past their monetary worth. Jewels, frequently alluded to as "a young lady's dearest companion," are exceptionally pursued and represent riches and extravagance. Their robbery was a blow not exclusively to the people in question yet in addition to the worldwide jewel exchange. The heist filled in as an obvious sign of the weaknesses in the security frameworks safeguarding valuable pearls and started discussions about the requirement for upgraded security in the business.

The vanishing of the taken fortunes from the Antwerp Precious stone Heist has produced an immense measure of hypothesis and interest. The daring execution of the heist and the lawbreakers' capacity to dodge catch have simply added to the persona of the taken merchandise. The effect of the heist, thusly, isn't restricted to the quick monetary misfortune however stretches out to the persevering through interest with strange violations and the appeal of brassy heists.

The secret encompassing the destiny of the taken fortunes has kept the story alive in the public's creative mind and in the realm of wrongdoing. In spite of broad examinations and a portion of those engaged with the heist being dealt with, a significant piece of the taken jewels stays absent, adding to the persevering through interest and effect of the Antwerp Precious stone Heist.

The Perplexing Problems of the Isabella Stewart Gardner Historical center Heist

The taken fortunes from the Isabella Stewart Gardner Exhibition hall heist in 1990 have been the subject of much investigation, both with regards to the workmanship world and the universe of wrongdoing. The heist, executed with fastidious preparation and daring execution, brought about the robbery of extremely valuable workmanship pieces worth an expected $500 million.

The effect of this strange heist is expansive. In the realm of workmanship, the taken fortunes' vanishing has made a void that won't be quickly filled. These pieces were not simply canvases; they were images of creative virtuoso and social legacy. The misfortune has been profoundly felt by workmanship fans, researchers, and the overall population, leaving an enduring effect on the craftsmanship world.

The monetary ramifications of the heist are likewise huge. The taken fortunes addressed a significant piece of the craftsmanship market's worth, and their vanishing brought up issues about the security and insurance of important social curios. The craftsmanship local area had to reexamine its safety efforts, prompting upgrades in the security of workmanship assortments around the world.

The Isabella Stewart Gardner Historical center heist's effect additionally reached out to the universe of wrongdoing. The dauntlessness and accuracy of the heist raised the crooks required to incredible status, and their story keeps on being a subject of interest. The persevering through secret of the taken fortunes keeps the universe of heists alive, exhibiting the expansive results of brassy lawbreaker activities.

In spite of broad examinations, the taken fortunes stay missing. The persevering through secret of the Isabella Stewart Gardner Exhibition hall heist keeps on catching the public's creative mind, filling in as a sign of the charm of perplexing wrongdoings and the getting through effect of daring heists.

The Investigation of the Hatton Nursery Heist Fortunes (2015)

The taken fortunes from the Hatton Nursery Heist in 2015, executed by a gathering of older lawbreakers known as the "Terrible Granddads," are a demonstration of the nervy execution of the heist and the effect it had on the universe of wrongdoing. The objective was the Hatton Nursery Safe Store Organization, situated in London's popular adornments area.

The taken fortunes comprised of money, adornments, and other important things, with an expected worth of £14 million. The effect of this heist is diverse, mirroring the dauntlessness of the lawbreakers and the results of their activities.

In the realm of wrongdoing, the brassy idea of the heist tested assumptions about the capacities of more established people. The tale of the "Terrible Granddads" has been a subject of interest, featuring the getting through charm of brassy heists and the obscured line among criminal and investigator.

The effect of the taken fortunes additionally stretched out to the survivors of the heist. The deficiency of important things and money was a huge catastrophe for the people who had shared their assets with the protected store organization. The heist brought up issues about the safety efforts set up and the weakness of such offices.

The outcome of the Hatton Nursery Heist brought about the worry of a large portion of the gangsters, who were dealt with. The effect of the heist, in this way, is a demonstration of the persevering quest for equity and the results of horrific acts.

In outline, the investigation of taken treasures from popular heists uncovers the multi-layered effect of bold crook attempts. Whether it's the persevering through secret of the Isabella Stewart Gardner Historical center heist, the interest with strange violations in the Antwerp Precious stone Heist, or the persevering through appeal of bold heists exemplified by the Hatton Nursery Heist, these taken fortunes keep on enrapturing the public's creative mind. The narratives of these heists and their repercussions feature the getting through effect of daringness, accuracy, and the constant quest for equity in the realm of wrongdoing.

Chapter 5

Pursuit and Justice

The pursuit and ensuing journey for equity are focal components in the repercussions of heists. In these high-stakes criminal undertakings, policing and examiners frequently set out on steady pursuits to catch the culprits and recuperate taken merchandise. This period of the heist story is set apart by its intricacy, challenges, and the persevering through battle to deal with the hoodlums.

The Incomparable Train Burglary (1963)

Following The Incomparable Train Burglary in 1963, a huge manhunt was sent off to deal with the pack of criminals. The daring heist, which saw the posse snatching £2.6 million, identical to over £50 million today, drew the consideration of policing both in the UK and globally.

The quest for the crooks included a broad examination and cooperation between different police powers. The gangsters, be that as it may, utilized strategies to dodge catch, like regularly changing their safe-houses and personalities. This wait-and-see game between the specialists and the posse brought about a few captures throughout the long term, however a significant number of the central participants figured out how to get away from catch.

One of the most remarkable captures was that of Ronnie Biggs, an individual from the group who had escaped the UK and gone through a very long time in different nations. Biggs' catch in Brazil in 1974 and his ensuing removal to the UK exhibited the getting through responsibility of policing deal with those associated with the heist.

The pursuit and journey for equity following The Incomparable Train Burglary is set apart by the getting through endeavors of policing, joint effort, and the intricacies of capturing crooks who utilized their boldness and sly to stay at large. The narrative of this popular heist fills in as a demonstration of the tenacious quest for equity, in any event, when the crooks appear to have vanished into the shadows.

The Isabella Stewart Gardner Gallery Heist (1990)

The quest for equity following the Isabella Stewart Gardner Gallery heist in 1990 is set apart by its continuous intricacy and the persevering through secret encompassing the taken fortunes. The nervy robbery, which saw the burglary of 13 precious crafts-manship pieces esteemed at around $500 million, prompted broad examinations by policing, both in the US and abroad.

In spite of a $10 million compensation for data prompting the recuperation of the taken workmanship, the compositions stay missing right up 'til now. The persevering through secret of the heist has created various hypotheses and theories about the whereabouts of the taken fortunes.

The quest for equity for this situation includes a two-overlap challenge: recuper-ating the taken craftsmanship and catching those dependable. The heist has become perhaps of the most popular perplexing wrongdoing in the realm of craftsmanship robbery, and the mission for equity keeps on being a subject of interest and interest.

The effect of the Isabella Stewart Gardner Historical center heist goes past the mon-etary misfortune. It highlights the getting through charm of perplexing wrongdoings and the persevering through responsibility of policing to deal with those included. The quest for equity for this situation fills in as a sign of the intricacies of examining venturesome heists and the difficulties of recuperating taken treasures.

The Banco Focal Thievery (2005)

The quest for equity following the Banco Focal Robbery in 2005 in Fortaleza, Brazil, gave policing a special test. The daring heist, which included digging a passage to get to the bank's vault and grabbing roughly 160 million Brazilian reais (around $70 million), left specialists bewildered.

The quest for equity included an enormous manhunt and broad examinations concerning the lawbreaker network behind the heist. In any case, the pack's capacity to sidestep catch was credited to their careful preparation and the clandestine idea of their passage activity.

Throughout the long term, a portion of the gangsters were captured and dealt with. Nonetheless, the persevering through secret of the taken cash, accepted to be covered up or washed, has made the quest for equity for this situation perplexing and testing.

The Banco Focal Robbery fills in as a demonstration of the dauntlessness and accuracy of heists, as well as the getting through battle to deal with hoodlums. The quest for those engaged with this heist is set apart by the interesting difficulties intro-duced by the lawbreakers' modern strategies and the getting through interest with nervy wrongdoings.

The Antwerp Jewel Heist (2003)

The quest for equity following the Antwerp Jewel Heist in 2003 was described by worldwide cooperation and the persevering endeavors to recuperate the taken dia-monds, gold, and valuable things esteemed at around $100 million. The daring heist in Antwerp, Belgium, designated the Antwerp Jewel Center, the core of the worldwide precious stone exchange.

The quest for equity included broad examinations, collaboration between policing in various nations, and a persevering quest for the lawbreakers. The daring execution of the heist, which included boring through different layers of safety, left examiners with an overwhelming test.

Large numbers of those engaged with the heist were secured and dealt with, however a huge part of the taken pearls stays missing. The persevering through secret of the destiny of the taken fortunes keeps on dazzling the public's creative mind and highlights the difficulties of recuperating taken products from brassy heists.

The quest for equity in the Antwerp Jewel Heist shows the worldwide extent of endeavors to deal with heist crooks and the intricacies of recuperating taken treasures. The getting through effect of this heist lies in the interest with strange problems and the continuous quest for equity.

The Hatton Nursery Heist (2015)

The quest for equity following the Hatton Nursery Heist in 2015, executed by a gathering of old crooks known as the "Terrible Granddads," involved the trepidation of the vast majority of the gangsters. The brassy heist designated the Hatton Nursery Safe Store Organization in London's eminent gems locale and brought about the robbery of an expected £14 million in real money, adornments, and different resources.

The quest for equity for this situation was set apart by the collaboration of policing and the use of cutting edge insightful strategies. The group's old age didn't keep them from falling under the examination of the law, and after some time, the majority of the gangsters were captured and dealt with.

The effect of the Hatton Nursery Heist lies chasing equity and the fruitful fear of the crooks. The heist tested assumptions about the abilities of more seasoned people in the realm of wrongdoing and the obscuring line among criminal and analyst.

5.1 Law enforcement efforts to track and capture criminals

Policing to track and catch crooks have developed altogether throughout the long term, driven by headways in innovation, changes in criminal way of behaving, and changes in cultural assumptions. The techniques and methodologies utilized by policing have become progressively modern, including a wide cluster of devices and procedures. This article investigates the multi-layered nature of policing, from conventional analytical techniques to state of the art mechanical methodologies, featuring the difficulties and moral contemplations that go with these endeavors.

One of the central apparatuses in policing is the analytical cycle. This interaction includes gathering data, breaking down proof, and building arguments against thought lawbreakers. Criminal investigators and examiners assume a critical part in this part of policing, their abilities and experience to sort out the riddle of crimes. Customary analytical methods like meetings, witness articulations, and reconnaissance keep on being fundamental parts of following and catching lawbreakers. These strategies depend on the assortment of actual proof, human insight, and other unmistakable hints to distinguish suspects and assemble arguments against them.

The advancement of legal science has upset the manner in which policing explore and settle wrongdoings. DNA examination, unique mark recognizable proof, ballistics, and other scientific methods have become pivotal apparatuses in distinguishing and catching lawbreakers. These strategies give substantial proof that can interface people to wrongdoings, prompting additional convictions and the expulsion of perilous guilty parties from society. The utilization of legal sciences has essentially expanded the achievement rate in addressing cold cases and recognizing already obscure crooks.

Besides, policing frequently work together with different associations and offices, both at the public and global levels. This collaboration assists in following and catching lawbreakers who with working across locales. The sharing of data, knowledge, and assets between organizations has become progressively significant in the present interconnected world. Interpol, Europol, and different worldwide police associations work with worldwide collaboration in policing, making it harder for hoodlums to avoid catch and equity.

Innovation significantly affects policing. The utilization of reconnaissance cameras, tag acknowledgment frameworks, and facial acknowledgment innovation has become predominant in numerous metropolitan regions. These devices assist policing with observing public spaces and track the developments of people. While these advances help in distinguishing and finding lawbreakers, they additionally raise worries about security and common freedoms. Finding some kind of harmony between open security and individual freedoms is really difficult for policing and society in general.

Web-based entertainment has likewise arisen as an important wellspring of data for following and catching lawbreakers. The far and wide utilization of stages like Facebook, Twitter, and Instagram has made a computerized impression for some people, including hoodlums. Policing frequently use web-based entertainment to assemble data about suspects, their partners, and their exercises. Be that as it may, this training isn't without its difficulties, as it includes exploring lawful and moral contemplations connected with online protection and information assortment.

Notwithstanding conventional analytical techniques and mechanical progressions, proactive policing systems have acquired noticeable quality lately. These methodologies include recognizing and focusing on regions with horror rates and conveying assets to stop crime. One such methodology is local area policing, which centers around building positive connections between policemen and the networks they serve. By encouraging trust and participation, local area policing expects to forestall wrongdoing and recognize crooks all the more really.

Prescient policing is another creative methodology that utilizes information investigation and AI calculations to figure where violations are probably going to happen. This system empowers policing to designate assets all the more proficiently and target regions with a higher gamble of crime. Be that as it may, prescient policing isn't without discussion, as it brings worries about predisposition up in information and algorithmic navigation.

While innovation has without a doubt improved policing, it has likewise led to new difficulties, like cybercrime. Hoodlums have adjusted to the computerized age, utilizing the web and innovation to commit different kinds of offenses, including hacking, data fraud, and online misrepresentation. Policing have needed to foster particular units and mastery to successfully battle cybercrime. These units work to follow computerized impressions, distinguish online crooks, and deal with them.

One more basic part of policing is the quest for outlaws and the execution of capture warrants. Organizations like the US Marshals Administration center around finding and catching people needed for different offenses. This work frequently includes joint effort with neighborhood policing and worldwide accomplices, as escapees can cross state and public lines to avoid catch. The fruitful following and catch of outlaws add to public security and the organization of equity.

Also, insight drove policing is a methodology that spotlights on get-together and dissecting data to forestall and tackle wrongdoings. This technique focuses on the proactive assortment and utilization of knowledge to distinguish criminal dangers and disturb criminal organizations. Insight drove policing stresses the significance of dividing data among organizations and wards, working with a more planned reaction to crimes.

One of the difficulties policing face in their endeavors to track and catch crooks is the rising complexity of criminal associations. Coordinated wrongdoing gatherings, including drug cartels, illegal exploitation organizations, and fear monger associations, work on a worldwide scale and utilize many-sided strategies to stay away from location. Policing should adjust and foster particular units to successfully battle these dangers. Worldwide collaboration and knowledge sharing are vital in battling transnational criminal associations.

The job of innovation in following and catching hoodlums couldn't possibly be more significant. The utilization of information bases, information mining, and prescient investigation has changed the manner in which policing work. Criminal data sets, for example, the FBI's Public Wrongdoing Data Center (NCIC) and the Mechanized Finger impression Distinguishing proof Framework (AFIS), give policing admittance to an abundance of data that can support recognizing and catching lawbreakers. These data sets store data on criminal accounts, warrants, missing people, and that's just the beginning, permitting policing rapidly access pivotal information during examinations.

Moreover, progresses in information mining and examination empower policing to distinguish examples and patterns in criminal way of behaving. By examining enormous datasets, policing gain experiences into the usual methodology of lawbreakers, assisting them with anticipating where and when violations are probably going to happen. This data is important in asset distribution and vital preparation.

Man-made consciousness (simulated intelligence) and AI have additionally extended policing in following and catching lawbreakers. Man-made intelligence calculations can deal with tremendous measures of information and distinguish important data rapidly. For instance, simulated intelligence can examine video film from reconnaissance cameras to perceive faces and tags, making it simpler to follow the developments of suspects. Simulated intelligence can likewise be utilized to investigate web-based entertainment information for proof connected with crimes or the whereabouts of suspects.

Facial acknowledgment innovation has been a subject of significant discussion with regards to policing. It empowers the speedy recognizable proof of people by contrasting their facial highlights with a data set of known people. While facial acknowledgment can be an integral asset for following and catching hoodlums, it has raised huge worries about security and common freedoms. Pundits contend that the innovation can prompt bogus up-sides, encroach on individual privileges, and be utilized for mass reconnaissance.

Biometric advancements stretch out past facial acknowledgment. Policing use unique mark acknowledgment, iris outputs, and voice acknowledgment to distinguish and follow people. These advancements have demonstrated significant in addressing violations and catching suspects. They are much of the time utilized in mix with different techniques to assemble bodies of evidence against hoodlums.

Reconnaissance innovation has developed essentially, with policing conveying a great many instruments to screen public spaces and track crooks. Shut circuit TV (CCTV) cameras are normally utilized in urban communities to dissuade wrongdoing and give significant proof in examinations. Tag acknowledgment frameworks consequently sweep and record the tags of vehicles, permitting policing track the developments of suspects. These advancements, when utilized dependably, can help policing find and catch lawbreakers.

Policing likewise utilize particular units and strategies to address explicit sorts of wrongdoing. For example, in the battle against drug dealing, offices frequently utilize secret tasks, sources, and wiretaps to accumulate proof and construct arguments against street pharmacists. These endeavors are important for a more extensive methodology to upset the medication exchange and secure those dependable.

In the domain of cybercrime, policing have laid out cybercrime units to research and arraign online wrongdoers. These units work with specialists in PC criminology and computerized examinations to follow the exercises of cybercriminals. The following and catching of online hoodlums frequently include worldwide participation, as numerous cybercriminals work from nations outside the ward of the researching organization.

One critical improvement lately has been the utilization of encryption in correspondence and information stockpiling. While encryption is a fundamental device for safeguarding the protection and security of people and associations, it can likewise present difficulties for policing. Encoded messages and records can be essentially impervious without the decoding key, making it challenging for policing to get to confirm in criminal examinations. This pressure among protection and policing for admittance to scrambled information stays a complex and developing issue.

The job of sources and spies in policing to track and catch crooks is one more area of interest. These people assume a pivotal part in social event knowledge and proof against criminal associations and suspects. Be that as it may, the utilization of witnesses and spies raises moral worries, as it might include people with criminal foundations or incite banters about ensnarement.

Moral contemplations are fundamental in policing to track and catch lawbreakers. Adjusting the need to catch guilty parties with the security of common freedoms and individual privileges is a continuous test. The utilization of innovation, reconnaissance, and information assortment techniques can encroach on protection and raise worries about the potential for misuse. Policing should lay out clear approaches and oversight systems to guarantee that these apparatuses are utilized capably and in consistence with the law.

Straightforwardness and responsibility are fundamental parts of moral policing. Responsibility systems, for example, body-worn cameras for cops and non military personnel oversight sheets, assist guarantee that policing are led as per laid out conventions and regard for residents' privileges. These actions additionally fabricate public trust and trust in policing.

Racial profiling and predisposition in policing been huge worries, especially with regards to following and catching crooks. The unbalanced focusing of racial and ethnic minorities has prompted calls for change and expanded investigation of policing. Organizations have been attempting to resolve these issues through preparing, strategy changes, and local area commitment endeavors.

The job of the overall set of laws in policing to track and catch lawbreakers is focal. Policing should accumulate proof, follow legitimate techniques, and regard people's privileges to guarantee that cases are prosecutable in court. The legitimate interaction, from getting court orders to directing cross examinations, should stick to the standards of fair treatment and established freedoms.

One outstanding test in policing is the harmony among security and common freedoms, especially with regards to counterterrorism. The post-9/11 time has seen an extension of reconnaissance and knowledge gathering endeavors to forestall psychological oppressor assaults. Notwithstanding, these endeavors have incited banters about the disintegration of common freedoms and the potential for overextend. The USA Loyalist Act and other regulation have extended policing for the sake of public safety, starting conversations about the requirement for governing rules.

Removal is a basic part of worldwide policing. Removal arrangements between nations consider the exchange of people blamed or sentenced for wrongdoings to confront equity in the mentioning country. The course of removal includes legitimate and conciliatory intricacies, as nations should explore their particular overall sets of laws and worldwide commitments. Removal is many times used to track and catch people who have escaped their nations of origin to keep away from arraignment.

Interpol, the Global Crook Police Association, assumes a crucial part in planning worldwide policing. Interpol fills in as a stage for part nations to share data and solicitation help with finding and catching criminals. This worldwide organization of policing upgrades the capacity to track and catch lawbreakers who cross global lines.

As of late, there has been a developing accentuation on supportive equity and local area based ways to deal with tending to criminal way of behaving. These methodologies center around fixing hurt, restoring wrongdoers, and including the local area all the while. Helpful equity programs intend to address the main drivers of criminal way of behaving and lessen recidivism. While these methodologies don't supplant conventional policing, they offer elective strategies for managing specific kinds of offenses.

Casualty promotion is one more fundamental part of policing. Supporting and offering types of assistance to wrongdoing casualties is a basic part of the law enforcement framework. Policing work in association with casualty backing associations to guarantee that casualties get the help they need, and their privileges are regarded all through the legitimate cycle.

All in all, policing to track and catch crooks are multi-layered, consolidating many apparatuses, techniques, and advancements. The analytical cycle, scientific science, innovation, and global participation all assume significant parts in recognizing and capturing hoodlums. Moral contemplations, responsibility, and legitimate protections are necessary to guaranteeing that policing are led inside the limits of the law and regard for individual freedoms. As innovation and criminal strategies keep on developing, policing should adjust and advance to address the difficulties of the cutting edge world while maintaining the standards of equity and public wellbeing.

5.2 International cooperation in solving heist cases

Global collaboration in settling heist cases is a mind boggling and diverse undertaking that requires coordination among policing, legislatures, and associations all over the planet. Heists, which include the burglary of important things, cash, or craftsmanship, frequently rise above public lines, making it significant for nations to cooperate to secure crooks and recuperate taken resources. This paper investigates the difficulties and advantages of global collaboration in settling heist cases, featuring the job of policing, offices, and worldwide associations in tending to these mind boggling crimes.

Heist cases, which can include high-stakes burglaries of craftsmanship, gems, or other important resources, have long caught the creative mind of the two lawbreakers and the overall population. These violations frequently require fastidious preparation, an organization of associates, and modern execution. Because of the critical worth of the taken products, heists present remarkable difficulties for policing and states. Such cases likewise present open doors for worldwide participation in finding and catching the culprits.

One of the essential difficulties in tackling heist cases is the portability of crooks and taken things across borders. Criminal associations engaged with heists frequently exploit the jurisdictional limits of individual nations, making it hard for policing to really seek after them. Worldwide participation is fundamental to conquer these moves and deal with heist wrongdoers.

The most important phase in worldwide participation includes dividing data and knowledge among policing from various nations. Interpol, the Global Crook Police Association, assumes a critical part in working with this trade of data. Interpol gives a stage to police powers overall to share information on crimes, including heists. This data sharing organization assists policing with distinguishing designs, track thinks, and recuperate taken property all the more successfully.

An eminent illustration of worldwide collaboration in tackling heist cases is the burglary of craftsmanship. Craftsmanship heists frequently include the unlawful dealing of significant artworks, models, and other social antiquities. Hoodlums might take these works of art and endeavor to offer them in various nations to keep away from identification. The Taken Craftsmanship Data set, kept up with by Interpol, aggregates data on taken works of art and helps policing in distinguishing and recuperating taken pieces. Exhibition halls, displays, and confidential gatherers can enlist their taken workmanship in the data set, making it open to policing around the world.

While worldwide participation through associations like Interpol is vital, it additionally requires the dynamic contribution of individual nations and their policing. Heists frequently require close coordination between the police, customs, and migration specialists. Nations should lay out systems for sharing basic data and proof connected with heist cases and crooks' developments.

Furthermore, lawful and conciliatory directs are fundamental in working with worldwide participation. Common lawful help deals (MLATs) and removal arrangements between nations empower the exchange of suspects and taken resources. These legitimate structures assume an essential part in heist examinations, guaranteeing that hoodlums can't dodge equity by crossing borders.

The recuperation of taken resources is a critical part of worldwide collaboration in heist cases. Crooks frequently endeavor to sell or move taken products across boundaries, and it is fundamental for track and hold onto these resources. Global associations like INTERPOL and UNESCO (the Assembled Countries Instructive, Logical and Social Association) work to localize taken social property. These associations, in a joint effort with policing, give direction on provenance research, debate goal, and the arrival of taken craftsmanships to their legitimate owners or nations.

Interpol's Show-stoppers Unit, laid out in 1947, is committed to tending to workmanship robbery and the unlawful exchange social property. This specific unit assists policing across the world with recuperating taken workmanship and ancient rarities. Interpol additionally teams up with associations like the Worldwide Committee of Galleries (ICOM) to advance collaboration between the police and the social legacy area.

One more critical test in global participation connected with heist cases is the need to fit lawful structures and strategies across various nations. Contrasting legitimate guidelines, proof prerequisites, and analytical conventions can convolute global endeavors to address heist cases. Nations should cooperate to make a typical structure that considers consistent joint effort in examinations and arraignments.

The requirement for normalization in worldwide participation turns out to be considerably more clear in cases including the burglary of uncommon and significant archeological antiques. These ancient rarities can be unlawfully unearthed and dealt across borders, making it moving for policing to follow and recuperate them. Worldwide associations, for example, UNESCO give rules to the security of social legacy and the counteraction of illegal dealing with social property. These rules assist nations with creating steady practices and lawful instruments to address the burglary and dealing of social antiquities.

Cross-line participation isn't restricted to cases including actual things like craftsmanship and adornments. Monetary wrongdoings connected with heists, for example, tax evasion and extortion, frequently have a worldwide aspect. Lawbreakers might utilize seaward records, shell organizations, and other monetary instruments to conceal the returns of heists. Global monetary organizations, similar to INTERPOL's Monetary Wrongdoings Unit, support policing in following and freezing resources related with heists and related monetary violations.

Cybercrime has likewise turned into a predominant part of heist cases, with lawbreakers utilizing modern hacking strategies to target monetary establishments, cryptographic money trades, and computerized resources. The borderless idea of the web and the obscurity it gives present critical difficulties to policing recognizing and catching cybercriminals. Global participation in network safety, including sharing danger knowledge and leading joint examinations, has become progressively essential in tending to digital related heists.

With regards to worldwide collaboration, data dividing and coordination among government organizations assume a basic part. Customs and movement specialists are much of the time engaged with the location of taken merchandise crossing borders. These offices work close by policing distinguish and capture taken things and secure people related with heists.

Furthermore, the association of political diverts is fundamental in tending to heist cases. Political missions can work with correspondence among legislatures and backing the removal of suspects to have to deal with penalties in the nation where the wrongdoing happened. In addition, discretionary strain can be applied to urge nations to coordinate completely in heist examinations, especially when worries about taken resources are being held in an unfamiliar locale.

The recuperation of taken resources is a focal part of worldwide collaboration in heist cases. Policing and associations cooperate to find, seize, and return taken property to its legitimate owners. In certain occurrences, taken resources might be held by people, associations, or nations that are not engaged with the robbery but rather have the taken things. Exchange and legitimate channels are frequently used to recuperate such resources.

One illustration of resource recuperation with regards to heist cases is the arrival of Nazi-stole from workmanship. After The Second Great War, incalculable fine arts were taken by the Nazis, and many wound up in the possession of gatherers, historical centers, or people all over the planet. Endeavors to recuperate and return these fine arts to their actual owners or their relatives have required worldwide collaboration, judicial procedures, and discussion. Associations like the Cases Gathering, which addresses Holocaust survivors and their main beneficiaries, have worked with legislatures and foundations to recognize and recuperate stole from craftsmanship.

The job of global associations in addressing heist cases isn't restricted to data sharing and resource recuperation. These associations likewise give preparing and limit building drives for policing and government authorities. Preparing projects can assist with working on the abilities and information on people engaged with heist examinations, improving them prepared to deal with complex cases that include global components.

INTERPOL, for example, offers a scope of preparing projects and instruments for policing around the world. These projects cover different parts of criminal examinations, including those connected with heist cases. Preparing centers around the most recent insightful methods, worldwide accepted procedures, and the utilization of INTERPOL's assets and data sets.

Furthermore, associations like Europol, the European Association's policing, assume a critical part in tending to heist cases inside the European Association. Europol offers help to EU part states in battling cross-line wrongdoing, including heists. It works with data sharing, knowledge examination, and joint activities to handle criminal associations associated with heists and resource robbery.

Europol likewise keeps up with data sets and apparatuses that help policing in following and distinguishing taken property. The Europol Taken Workmanship Data set, for example, contains data on taken craftsmanship and social antiques and can be gotten to by policing across the EU.

With regards to worldwide participation, the job of private associations and specialists can't be undervalued. Confidential examiners, craftsmanship recuperation firms, and security organizations frequently team up with policing and legislatures to aid heist cases. These specialists offer specific information and assets that would be useful, helping with the recuperation of taken resources and the distinguishing proof of suspects.

For instance, associations like the Workmanship Misfortune Register keep up with data sets of taken craftsmanship and curios. Workmanship Misfortune Register works with policing, displays, and authorities to help distinguish and recuperate taken things. It additionally aids an expected level of effort processes for workmanship exchanges, decreasing the gamble of obtaining taken craftsmanship.

The confidential area likewise assumes a part in network protection endeavors connected with heist cases. Network safety firms and PC legal sciences specialists are frequently called upon to research digital related heists and give aptitude in recognizing and following cybercriminals. The participation among public and confidential associations is fundamental in tending to the consistently advancing difficulties presented by cybercrime.

Interdisciplinary participation is fundamental in tackling heist cases that include different components, including workmanship burglary, monetary violations, online protection, and line intersections. Specialists from various fields, like policing, craftsmanship history, criminal science, network safety, and strategy, should cooperate to foster extensive systems for following and catching heist culprits.

On account of workmanship robbery, provenance research assumes a critical part. Workmanship antiquarians and specialists team up with policing associations like Interpol to follow the set of experiences and responsibility for fine arts. Provenance exploration can assist with deciding the genuine proprietors of the taken workmanship and give basic proof in criminal examinations.

The association of legitimate specialists is major in exploring the complex lawful scene of worldwide collaboration. Attorneys and legitimate researchers work to guarantee that removal, resource recuperation, and other lawful cycles are directed as per worldwide regulation and the general sets of laws of the nations in question.

The job of the scholarly world in heist cases isn't restricted to provenance research. Crime analysts and specialists in the field of wrongdoing anticipation can add to the advancement of techniques to prevent heists and break down examples of criminal way of behaving. Their experiences can assist policing with bettering figure out the inspirations and strategies of heist lawbreakers.

In rundown, worldwide collaboration in tackling heist cases is a multi-layered and testing try that requires coordination among policing, government substances, global associations, and confidential specialists. Heist cases frequently include the robbery of significant resources, including craftsmanship, gems, and cash, and may have a worldwide aspect, making it essential for nations to cooperate to track and catch lawbreakers and recuperate taken things. The job of associations like Interpol, Europol, and UNESCO is instrumental in working with data sharing, resource recuperation, and limit building. Political channels, legitimate systems, and confidential area coordinated effort additionally assume huge parts in settling heist cases. Cross-disciplinary participation, including specialists from different fields, is fundamental in tending to the complicated parts of heist examinations. Worldwide collaboration not just upgrades the capacity to track and catch heist culprits yet in addition safeguards social legacy, recuperate taken resources, and deal with hoodlums on a worldwide scale.

5.3 The challenges and triumphs of bringing heist perpetrators to justice

The difficulties and wins of dealing with heist culprits are at the center of the law enforcement framework's continuous fight against robberies of significant resources, like craftsmanship, adornments, and cash. Heists are mind boggling violations that frequently include fastidious preparation, worldwide aspects, and the burglary of high-esteem things. As policing, legislatures, and associations cooperate to catch heist culprits, a horde of hindrances and victories are experienced en route.

Heists have for some time been a subject of interest for the two lawbreakers and the overall population. These high-stakes wrongdoings frequently include trying burglaries that catch the creative mind, whether it's a multimillion-dollar craftsmanship heist, an intricate gems burglary, or a complex bank robbery. Be that as it may, the truth of these cases is a long way from the exciting depictions found in films and media. The quest for heist culprits and the recuperation of taken resources are testing tries that require worldwide participation, complex insightful methods, and a comprehension of the special parts of these violations.

One of the essential difficulties in dealing with heist culprits is the complicated preparation and execution of these violations. Heists are not normally unconstrained demonstrations; they include broad planning, coordination among hoodlums, and, on occasion, a point by point information on security frameworks. These attributes make heists challenging to forestall and examine. Hoodlums might go through months or even years exploring and arranging a heist, concentrating on their objectives, and recognizing weaknesses in safety efforts.

The degree of refinement in heist cases differs generally. A few heists include elaborate plans, for example, the robbery of extremely valuable fine arts from exhibition halls, in which hoodlums may enter various layers of safety. Conversely, others might include basic however top notch burglaries of gems stores or reinforced trucks. No matter what the degree of complexity, heist culprits frequently abandon negligible proof, making it moving for policing distinguish and secure them.

Global aspects further entangle heist cases. Crooks who do heists frequently exploit the limits of purviews, which can represent a critical snag to examinations. For instance, a crook might commit a heist in one nation and afterward transport taken resources across borders, making it challenging for nearby policing to find them. Global participation is fundamental to beat these jurisdictional obstructions and deal with heist culprits.

Besides, the high worth of taken resources, whether it's extremely valuable craftsmanship or a vault loaded with cash, makes heists alluring to criminal associations. These associations frequently have broad assets, organizations, and the capacity to work across borders. Their association can altogether build the intricacy of heist cases and require policing to likewise adjust their procedures and assets.

The requirement for worldwide collaboration is clear when heists include the dealing of taken resources. Hoodlums frequently endeavor to offer or move taken things across lines to discard them and keep away from recognition. These resources can circle in different nations, going through the hands of various people and associations. Following and holding onto these taken resources become foremost in heist examinations.

One outstanding illustration of worldwide collaboration in heist cases is the robbery of work of art. Workmanship heists present novel difficulties, as taken craftsmanships can be exchanged on the bootleg market and change hands on different occasions. Criminal associations might utilize go-betweens, making layers of intricacy in following taken craftsmanship. Global associations, like Interpol, have laid out specific data sets, similar to the Taken Workmanship Data set, to index taken fine arts and help policing in distinguishing and recuperating them.

Interpol assumes a significant part in working with global collaboration by giving a stage to police powers overall to share data on crimes, including heists. The association's organization empowers policing to cooperate, recognize examples, and track suspects across borders. This data sharing cycle can prompt leap forwards in examinations and the ID of heist culprits.

Resource recuperation is one more huge part of worldwide collaboration in heist cases. Lawbreakers might endeavor to stow away, sell, or move taken resources for various purviews, making the following and capture of these resources a complicated undertaking. Worldwide associations, like INTERPOL and UNESCO, give direction and backing to the bringing home of taken resources, especially in cases including social property.

The arrival of taken social property, whether it's craft plundered during furnished clashes or authentic curios taken from historical centers, requires global cooperation. Associations like UNESCO work to safeguard social legacy and forestall the illegal dealing of social property. They give rules and assets to nations to foster reliable practices and legitimate systems to address the robbery and dealing of social relics. These endeavors assist with taking taken resources back to their actual owners or nations.

Notwithstanding the difficulties, there are a few vital components to consider while attempting to deal with heist culprits. These incorporate successful policing, resource recuperation, and legitimate instruments.

Policing should utilize a multi-layered approach while examining heist cases. Collaboration and coordination between various offices, like the police, customs, migration, and monetary establishments, are vital. Heist cases frequently require cross-line joint effort, and these offices assume an essential part in distinguishing, following, and capturing heist culprits.

Preparing and limit building are fundamental to improving the abilities and information on policing associated with heist examinations. Global associations like INTERPOL offer preparation programs that cover different parts of criminal examinations, including those connected with heists. These projects give policing most recent insightful methods, global prescribed procedures, and the utilization of INTERPOL's assets and information bases.

Cybercrime has turned into an undeniably critical part of heist cases, with law-breakers utilizing modern hacking procedures to target monetary foundations, cryptographic money trades, and advanced resources. The borderless idea of the web and the obscurity it gives present critical difficulties in recognizing and catching cybercriminals. Global collaboration in network protection, including sharing danger knowledge and leading joint examinations, is fundamental in tending to digital related heists.

Also, lawful and discretionary diverts are central in working with global collaboration in heist cases. Common lawful help settlements (MLATs) and removal arrangements between nations empower the exchange of suspects and taken resources. These legitimate structures assume an essential part in heist examinations, guaranteeing that crooks can't sidestep equity by crossing borders. Discretionary missions likewise aid correspondence among legislatures and backing the removal of suspects.

The contribution of legitimate specialists is fundamental in exploring the complex lawful scene of worldwide collaboration. Attorneys and legitimate researchers work to guarantee that removal, resource recuperation, and other legitimate cycles are led as per global regulation and the general sets of laws of the nations in question.

The job of private associations and specialists in heist cases isn't restricted to workmanship recuperation or confidential examination. The confidential area, including craftsmanship recuperation firms, network safety organizations, and confidential agents, frequently teams up with policing and states to aid heist examinations. These specialists offer particular information and assets that might be of some value, helping with the recuperation of taken resources and the ID of suspects.

For instance, craftsmanship recuperation firms work close by policing to distinguish and recuperate taken fine arts, frequently utilizing provenance examination and exchange abilities. Confidential examiners can give experiences into complex heist cases, for example, the robbery of important adornments or the character of suspects engaged with the wrongdoing. Network safety organizations and PC criminology specialists assume a significant part in examining digital related heists and recognizing cybercriminals.

The recuperation of taken resources is a focal component of global participation in heist cases. In many examples, taken resources might be held by people, associations, or nations that are not engaged with the robbery but rather have the taken things. Exchange and legitimate channels are frequently used to recuperate these resources.

One illustration of resource recuperation with regards to heist cases is the arrival of Nazi-stole from workmanship. After The Second Great War, incalculable fine arts were taken by the Nazis, and many wound up in the possession of gatherers, historical centers, or people all over the planet. Endeavors to recuperate and return these fine arts to their actual owners or their relatives have required worldwide collaboration, official procedures, and discussion.

The contribution of the confidential area, especially workmanship recuperation firms and concentrated law offices, has been instrumental in the arrival of Nazi-stole from craftsmanship. These associations team up with state run administrations, establishments, and people to distinguish stole from craftsmanship, haggle with current holders, and guarantee the compensation of these social fortunes.

In the domain of craftsmanship recuperation, provenance research assumes a huge part in deciding the set of experiences and responsibility for fine arts. Craftsmanship students of history and specialists team up with policing, state run administrations, and associations to follow the provenance of taken workmanship. Provenance examination can assist with deciding the genuine proprietors of the taken workmanship and give basic proof in criminal examinations.

One more victory in dealing with heist culprits lies in the fruitful recuperation of taken resources that have been sold or moved to people, associations, or nations not straightforwardly associated with the robbery. Lawful instruments, for example, court requests and peaceful accords, are utilized to work with the arrival of these resources for their actual owners.

Social legacy safeguarding is another region where achievement can be accomplished. Endeavors to secure and localize taken social property, whether it's craft plundered during clashes or verifiable ancient rarities taken from galleries, show worldwide coordinated effort. These endeavors assist with reestablishing taken social property to its legitimate owners or nations, saving the world's social legacy.

The recuperation of taken resources isn't restricted to craftsmanship however reaches out to different other important things, including gems, ancient pieces, and authentic relics. Resource recuperation drives require a mix of legitimate, conciliatory, and investigatory endeavors, frequently including policing, states, and associations.

One eminent accomplishment in dealing with heist culprits is the catch and arraignment of the people answerable for high-profile heists. Now and again, fastidious insightful work, worldwide collaboration, and creative strategies lead to the ID and fear of heist culprits. The fruitful indictment of these lawbreakers fills in as an impediment to future heist endeavors and sends areas of strength for a that such wrongdoings won't be tolerated.

The arrival of taken resources for their actual owners or nations is another huge victory. Whether it includes workmanship, gems, or verifiable relics, the rebuilding of these things addresses a triumph for equity and the safeguarding of social legacy. Examples of overcoming adversity in resource recuperation frequently include steady endeavors, talks, and legitimate components that guarantee the taken things are gotten back to their legitimate spot.

Furthermore, progress in the counteraction of heists should be visible as a victory. Further developed safety efforts, worldwide collaboration, and public mindfulness have added to the prevention of heist endeavors. By tending to weaknesses and improving security, policing and associations can decrease the potential open doors for crooks to complete fruitful heists.

The recuperation of resources in cases including Nazi-stole from craftsmanship is an illustration of worldwide participation prompting huge victories. Endeavors to distinguish and return craftsmanship plundered during The Second Great War have brought about the compensation of incalculable works of art to their actual owners or their relatives. Global associations, state run administrations, confidential specialists, and legitimate systems play played urgent parts in these victories.

Participation among state run administrations and global associations, like INTERPOL and UNESCO, has additionally prompted various victories in social property compensation. Taken social ancient rarities have been gotten back to their nations of beginning, and lawful structures have been laid out to forestall unlawful dealing with social property.

Forestalling future heists is a continuous test, yet victories can be accomplished through the turn of events and execution of safety efforts and practices. Exhibition halls, displays, and confidential gatherers have put resources into security improvements to safeguard their significant workmanship and ancient rarities. Innovation, including further developed reconnaissance frameworks and computerized listing of social property, plays had an impact in forestalling robbery and working with the recuperation of taken resources.

While the difficulties of dealing with heist culprits are huge, the victories exhibit the flexibility and assurance of policing, state run administrations, associations, and people in the battle against burglaries of significant resources. Global collaboration, creative analytical procedures, lawful components, and public mindfulness have all added to advance in tending to heist cases.

The difficulties and wins of dealing with heist culprits highlight the intricacy and uniqueness of these crook cases. Heists are portrayed by their fastidious preparation, global aspects, and the high worth of taken resources. These components make heist examinations requesting and frequently require creative systems, coordinated effort, and the use of different assets.

Global participation is fundamental in defeating the jurisdictional hindrances presented by heist cases. Hoodlums who commit heists frequently exploit the limits of nations, requiring joint effort among policing, state run administrations, and associations around the world. Data sharing, resource recuperation, and the execution of legitimate components are central in tending to these complicated cases.

Policing should utilize a complex methodology that includes coordination between various organizations, including police, customs, movement, and monetary establishments. Preparing and limit building are fundamental for upgrading the abilities and information on people engaged with heist examinations. The inclusion of the confidential area, including workmanship recuperation firms, network safety organizations, and confidential examiners, adds significant skill and assets to these cases.

The fruitful recuperation of taken resources and the recognizable proof and arraignment of heist culprits address critical victories in the fight against these wrongdoings. These victories frequently require steady endeavors, legitimate instruments, and worldwide collaboration. Also, the counteraction of heists is a continuous test, however headway can be made through improved safety efforts, innovation, and public mindfulness.

Chapter 6

Unsolved Mysteries

Inexplicable problems have long held an interest for mankind. These confounding cases, portrayed by their absence of goal, have aroused the interest of people, agents, and the public the same. Whether they include vanishings, unexplained peculiarities, or perplexing wrongdoings, inexplicable problems challenge how we might interpret the world and the constraints of human information. In this paper, we will dive into the universe of strange problems, investigating the absolute most popular cases, the difficulties they present, and the persevering through interest they hold.

Perplexing problems arrive in different structures, from unexplained peculiarities to puzzling vanishings and strange violations. A few secrets, similar to the Loch Ness Beast or Bigfoot, include tricky animals that have caught the public's creative mind for ages. These cases frequently depend on recounted proof, observer records, and fables, making them trying to research through conventional logical techniques.

Different secrets rotate around mysterious occasions, for example, the Tunguska occasion of 1908. For this situation, a monstrous blast happened in a distant area of Siberia, straightening more than 2,000 square kilometers of timberland. Regardless of broad exploration, the reason for the blast stays a subject of discussion, with hypotheses going from shooting star effect on a mysterious government try.

Furthermore, perplexing vanishings, similar to the instance of Malaysia Aircrafts Flight 370, have puzzled examiners and the general population. In 2014, the airplane disappeared in transit from Kuala Lumpur to Beijing, with no convincing proof of its destiny. Broad ventures in the Indian Sea have yielded some destruction, however the plane's vanishing remains covered in vulnerability.

Strange violations additionally structure a huge classification of secrets, with cases like the Dark Dahlia murder in 1947 charming general society. The merciless killing of Elizabeth Short, whose body was viewed as cut off down the middle and disfigured, stays one of the most well known strange homicide cases ever. Regardless of various examinations and innumerable speculations, the personality of the executioner and the intention behind the wrongdoing have never not entirely settled.

The Zodiac Executioner, who threatened Northern California in the last part of the 1960s and mid 1970s, is another scandalous perplexing homicide case. The executioner provoked police and the media with mysterious letters and codes, further confusing the examination. While there have been suspects and hypotheses, the genuine personality of the Zodiac Executioner stays obscure.

Numerous inexplicable problems become social peculiarities, rousing books, films, narratives, and novice investigators who endeavor to unwind the conundrum. These cases frequently resist traditional clarifications, and the shortfall of conclusion energizes perpetual hypothesis and interest.

While perplexing problems can be unendingly entrancing, they likewise represent a few difficulties for examiners and the quest for truth. These difficulties envelop different angles, including the absence of actual proof, untrustworthy onlooker accounts, the progression of time, and the consistently present impact of fables and metropolitan legends.

One critical test in strange problems is the shortage of cement actual proof. Without substantial hints, like DNA, fingerprints, or measurable proof, specialists face a difficult task in sorting out the riddle. For instance, in cases including unexplained peculiarities or slippery animals like Bigfoot or the Loch Ness Beast, the shortfall of actual proof upsets endeavors to lay out the presence of these confounding creatures.

In perplexing vanishings, the absence of actual proof can particularly disappoint. At the point when people disappear suddenly, there are much of the time no pieces of information abandoned to show their whereabouts or destiny. This shortfall of unmistakable proof gains it unimaginably testing to gain ground in examinations and eventually tackle these secrets.

Another critical test emerges from untrustworthy observer accounts. Memory is error prone, and the progression of time can twist memories of occasions or people. Onlooker declaration, which is much of the time a basic part of examinations, can be conflicting and loaded with mistakes. In high-profile cases, the media and public consideration can additionally muddle the unwavering quality of onlooker accounts, as people might be affected by outside variables or anxious to add to the story.

The scandalous instance of the Loch Ness Beast outlines the test of temperamental observer accounts. Throughout the long term, various individuals have revealed seeing a huge, unidentified animal in Loch Ness, Scotland. Be that as it may, the depictions and subtleties of these sightings shift generally, and many records need validating proof. The Loch Ness Beast stays a strange problem to a great extent because of the untrustworthy idea of observer declaration for this situation.

The progression of time is one more obstacle in settling perplexing problems. As years transform into many a long time into hundreds of years, proof might disintegrate or get derailed, witnesses die, and the path develops cold. In authentic perplexing cases, the restricted accessibility of contemporary records and the failure to address living observers present critical deterrents to accomplishing goal.

For example, on account of the Tunguska occasion of 1908, the absence of prompt logical examination has made it trying to conclusively decide the reason for the blast. Scientists have needed to depend on authentic records, observer records, and restricted actual proof, which are all dependent upon the impediments of time.

The impact of old stories and metropolitan legends can likewise convolute inexplicable problems. These stories frequently sustain fantasies and misguided judgments, making it hard to recognize reality from fiction. Now and again, the lines among legend and reality become obscured, preventing endeavors to uncover reality.

On account of the Loch Ness Beast, long stretches of legends and melodrama have added to an intricate snare of stories, photos, and accounts that may not line up with the real world. Figuring out the layers of fantasy and old stories to show up at an unmistakable comprehension of the secret is a considerable errand.

Regardless of these difficulties, perplexing problems keep on enrapturing the general population, moving interest, banter, and a feeling of marvel. Generally speaking, the persevering through appeal of these secrets lies in the very reality that they stay perplexing, leaving space for hypothesis, creative mind, and the chance of revelation.

Beginner detectives and easy chair examiners play had a huge impact in endeavoring to unwind strange problems. The web and the approach of online networks have empowered fans to team up, share data, and propose hypotheses. These novice endeavors can prompt new viewpoints and bits of knowledge, at times reigniting revenue in cool cases and provoking new examinations.

One striking illustration of beginner sleuthing is the situation of the Brilliant State Executioner. The character of this productive chronic attacker and killer escaped policing many years. Be that as it may, the case encountered an advancement when novice specialist Michelle McNamara started exploring and expounding on the violations. Her work, alongside the endeavors of different agents and the utilization of public family history data sets, at last prompted the capture and conviction of the Brilliant State Executioner.

Perplexing problems have additionally filled in as the motivation for endless books, films, and narratives. These imaginative works frequently investigate potential answers for the secrets or rethink the occasions. While fictionalized records may not give substantial responses, they offer crowds a chance to draw in with the secrets and think about alternate points of view.

For instance, the Dark Dahlia murder has been the subject of various books, movies, and TV series. These works draw on the genuine case while integrating components of show, tension, and hypothesis. While they may not give a conclusive goal, they add to the continuous talk encompassing the secret.

The persevering through allure of inexplicable problems likewise reaches out to the universe of science and the scholarly community. Specialists in different fields, including paleontology, history, and material science, frequently research strange peculiarities looking for replies. Their work might include reevaluating proof, directing examinations, or growing new hypotheses to reveal insight into these secrets.

The instance of the Tunguska occasion represents the logical way to deal with perplexing problems. Specialists and researchers keep on concentrating on the occasion, directing examinations and breaking down information to acquire a superior comprehension of the blast's goal. While the secret remaining parts strange, the logical quest for information stays a main thrust in the examination.

Inexplicable problems can likewise act as useful examples and wellsprings of motivation. They help us to remember the restrictions of human information and the getting through feeling of marvel that secrets can incite. These cases empower interest, decisive reasoning, and the quest for replies, even despite apparently difficult difficulties.

In certain examples, perplexing problems have propelled people to seek after professions in fields like analytical reporting, policing, logical exploration. The unsettled idea of these secrets energizes a feeling of request and an appreciation for the quest for truth.

While perplexing problems stay a dazzling part of human interest and request, they likewise act as a wake up call of the requirement for logical meticulousness, decisive reasoning, and proof based examination. In a world loaded up with complex inquiries and riddles, the quest for truth and information is a central human undertaking.

Perplexing problems catch our creative mind, challenge how we might interpret the world, and motivate interest. These mysterious cases, going from unexplained peculiarities to perplexing wrongdoings, have entranced mankind for a really long time. While they present huge difficulties to examiners and scientists, they likewise act as a demonstration of the persevering through mission for information and truth.

Inexplicable problems take different structures, with each sort introducing its novel arrangement of difficulties and interest. Peculiarities like the Loch Ness Beast and Bigfoot, described by tricky animals and narrative proof, have charmed the public's creative mind for ages. These cases frequently depend on observer records, old stories, and an absence of cement logical proof.

Unexplained occasions, for example, the Tunguska occasion of 1908, represent an alternate kind of secret. In these cases, an unexpected and horrendous event challenges quick clarification, passing on researchers and scientists to conjecture on the reason. Regardless of broad examinations, reality behind these occasions might stay tricky.

Perplexing vanishings, similar to the puzzling disappearing of Malaysia Carriers Flight 370 out of 2014, altogether affect public awareness. The shortfall of indisputable proof in regards to the destiny of the airplane has energized broad quests and examinations. Be that as it may, the plane's vanishing stays quite possibly of the most confounding and strange case in aeronautics history.

Inexplicable wrongdoings, for example, the Dark Dahlia murder and the Zodiac Executioner, address the absolute most renowned perplexing problems. These cases include egregious wrongdoings, secretive interchanges, and slippery culprits. In spite of various examinations and speculations, these secrets keep on escaping goal, propagating public interest.

Challenges in settling strange problems are complex and envelop different parts of examination and exploration. The absence of cement actual proof represents a critical obstacle, especially in cases including slippery animals, unexplained peculiarities, and secretive vanishings. Without a trace of substantial hints like DNA or criminological proof, examiners face trouble in gaining ground.

Untrustworthy observer accounts add one more layer of intricacy to perplexing problems. Memory is dependent upon bending, and the progression of time can disintegrate the exactness of memories. Onlooker declaration, frequently a urgent component of examinations, might be conflicting and impacted by outer elements, media consideration, or melodrama.

The progression of time itself presents a considerable test. As years transform into long stretches of time, authentic inexplicable cases become considerably more hard to examine. The deficiency of contemporary records, the failure to address living observers, and the weakening of proof ruin progress in figuring out these secrets.

The impact of old stories and metropolitan legends further entangles strange problems. These accounts frequently obscure the lines among truth and fiction, making it trying to perceive reality. Cases like the Loch Ness Beast are encircled by layers of legend, fables, and drama, darkening the center of the secret.

Novice detectives and easy chair examiners play had a critical impact in the mission to settle strange problems. Online people group and discussions give a stage to fans to team up, share data, and propose hypotheses. Their commitments can prompt new points of view, revive cold cases, and brief new examinations.

The job of media and imaginative works, including books, motion pictures, and narratives, couldn't possibly be more significant in that frame of mind of strange problems. These works frequently investigate potential arrangements or reconsider the occasions. While they may not give authoritative responses, they connect with crowds, energize decisive reasoning, and sustain the interest encompassing these secrets.

The persevering through charm of perplexing problems lies in the very truth that they stay unsettled, leaving space for hypothesis, creative mind, and the chance of disclosure. While challenges persevere, the getting through allure of these secrets powers a feeling of marvel, request, and the quest for replies.

The logical and scholarly networks additionally draw in with strange problems, directing examination and examinations to disentangle puzzlers. Scientists from different fields, including prehistoric studies, history, and physical science, look to reveal insight into these secrets. While not all cases might be conclusively settled, the quest for information stays a main thrust in the examination.

Perplexing problems rouse people to seek after vocations in fields like analytical news coverage, policing, logical exploration. The secrets empower a feeling of request, decisive reasoning, and an appreciation for the quest for truth.

6.1 Stories of heists that remain unsolved or treasures not yet recovered

The charm of heists and secret fortunes has entranced individuals for a really long time. These charming stories frequently include brassy robberies and tricky fortunes, with lawbreakers leaving not many follows and specialists confronting an overwhelming test. In this exposition, we will dig into the universe of heists and fortunes that stay strange or unseen, investigating the absolute most spellbinding cases, the secrets that cover them, and the getting through interest they hold.

Heists and secret fortunes come in different structures, with each case introducing its one of a kind arrangement of difficulties and interest. These accounts frequently include critical burglaries of significant resources, like craftsmanship, valuable pearls, authentic ancient rarities, or enormous amounts of cash. The intentions behind these violations differ, from monetary benefit and individual enhancement to philosophical inspirations or even the longing for reputation.

Quite possibly of the most notable and puzzling heist in history is the burglary of the Isabella Stewart Gardner Historical center in 1990. Two men dressed as cops entered the exhibition hall in Boston, Massachusetts, and took 13 bits of workmanship esteemed at around $500 million. The taken fine art included magnum opuses by specialists like Vermeer, Rembrandt, and Degas. In spite of many years of examinations, the taken pieces stay missing, and the case is viewed as one of the biggest strange workmanship heists on the planet.

The Gardner Gallery heist features the difficulties examiners face when significant craftsmanship is taken. The bootleg market for taken craftsmanship is tremendous and frequently covered in mystery, making it hard to follow the development of taken pieces. Criminal associations might hold important works of art for payment or offer them to private authorities who will address extreme costs for such fortunes. The recuperation of taken craftsmanship can be a mind boggling and extensive cycle, and by and large, the taken pieces are always avoided their legitimate owners or galleries.

Another famous heist case includes the robbery of $70 million worth of jewels, gold, and other valuable pearls from the Antwerp Precious stone Place in 2003. A gathering of Italian criminals, known as the "School of Turin," executed the heist, which included bypassing numerous layers of safety. The taken jewels and other valuable stones were rarely recuperated, and the heist stays one of the biggest jewel burglaries ever.

The Antwerp Precious stone Place heist is a demonstration of the dauntlessness and complexity of heist crooks. Hoodlums engaged with such high-stakes wrongdoings frequently utilize careful preparation, exploit weaknesses in security frameworks, and have the skill to dodge catch. Worldwide collaboration is fundamental in tending to heists with a global aspect, as hoodlums may ship taken resources across lines to stay away from recognition.

The Lufthansa heist at John F. Kennedy Global Air terminal in 1978 is one more unbelievable case in the realm of heists. A gathering of crooks, purportedly organized by James Burke (otherwise called "Jimmy the Gent"), took roughly $5 million in real money and almost $1 million in gems from the Lufthansa freight terminal. The hoodlums were exceptionally coordinated and abandoned negligible proof. Right up 'til now, a large part of the taken money and gems has never been recuperated, and the case stays quite possibly of the most renowned strange heist ever.

The Lufthansa heist, broadly depicted in the film "Goodfellas," outlines the degree of mystery and heartlessness frequently connected with heist cases. The crooks engaged with such tasks are normally very much associated, making it challenging for policing accumulate data from likely observers or witnesses. The taken money and adornments might have been laundered through different channels, making them almost difficult to follow.

Notwithstanding heists including actual resources, digital heists have become progressively predominant in the advanced age. The robbery of digital money, specifically, has caught the consideration of crooks and policing. One of the most prominent cases is the burglary of 850,000 bitcoins from the now-dead cryptographic money trade Mt. Gox in 2014. The taken bitcoins, esteemed at billions of dollars, have never been completely recuperated, and the case highlights the one of a kind difficulties presented by cybercrime and computerized resources.

The Mt. Gox case features the namelessness and worldwide reach of cybercriminals. Cryptographic forms of money offer a degree of secrecy that conventional monetary exchanges don't, making it hard to follow the development of taken computerized resources. The worldwide idea of digital currency trades adds one more layer of intricacy, as these stages can work across global boundaries. Global participation in cybercrime examinations is urgent in tending to such cases.

Rather than heists, stowed away fortunes frequently include important resources that have been purposefully hidden, frequently because of reasons going from wartime plundering to antiquated internment rehearses. These fortunes, whether they comprise of gold, gems, or verifiable curios, catch the creative mind and light the longing for revelation. Nonetheless, they can stay concealed for a really long time, challenging endeavors at recuperation.

The story of the Golden Room, in some cases called the "Eighth Marvel of the World," is one of the most popular accounts of a buried fortune. The Golden Room was a rich chamber in the Catherine Castle of Tsarskoye Selo close to St. Petersburg, Russia, decorated with golden boards, gold leaf, and valuable diamonds. During The Second Great War, the Nazis stole from the room, and in spite of broad endeavors to recuperate it, the Golden Room stays missing. The secret of its whereabouts has persevered for quite a long time, with hypotheses going from it being lost to being concealed in distant areas.

The Golden Room's vanishing brings up issues about the destiny of fortunes plundered during furnished clashes. The tumult of war, combined with the purposeful activities of thieves, has brought about the deficiency of endless verifiable curios and resources. A portion of these fortunes have been recuperated throughout the long term, while others stay tricky, stowed away or lost to time.

The quest for buried prizes likewise stretches out to the universe of paleontology. The journey for antiquated civilizations and their lost urban communities has spellbound travelers and scientists for a really long time. One such unbelievable city is the lost city of El Dorado, frequently connected with a mythical brilliant city found some place in the unknown domains of South America. Notwithstanding various undertakings and investigations, El Dorado stays unseen, filling in as an image of the persevering through charm of stowed away fortunes.

In the domain of submerged treasures, the disaster area of the Spanish ship Nuestra Señora de Atocha sticks out. The boat, loaded down with valuable pearls, silver, gold, and different resources, sank off the bank of Florida in 1622 during a tropical storm. For quite a long time, treasure trackers scoured the oceans looking for the Atocha's freight. During the 1980s, the destruction was at last found, and a critical piece of the fortune was recuperated, yet a significant sum remains unfound. The mission for the excess bits of the Atocha's freight represents the difficulties and compensations of submerged treasure hunting.

The persevering through interest with stowed away fortunes lies in the excitement of disclosure and the potential for impossible riches. These stories frequently include secretive guides, legends, and investigations into remote and hazardous areas. While certain fortunes have been effectively recuperated, many stay disguised, igniting the creative mind and rousing travelers to proceed with their journeys.

Challenges in tackling heists and recuperating stowed away fortunes are complex, enveloping different perspectives, including the absence of actual proof, the impact of fables and legends, the progression of time, and the worldwide element of many cases.

One critical test in settling heists is the shortage of cement actual proof. Without substantial hints, like DNA, fingerprints, or legal proof, agents face a daunting struggle in sorting out the riddle. Hoodlums frequently abandon not many follows, especially in carefully arranged and executed heists. The shortfall of actual proof impedes endeavors to recognize the culprits and recuperate taken resources.

The impact of old stories and legends can likewise convolute heist cases. These stories frequently sustain fantasies and misguided judgments, making it challenging to observe truth from fiction. Now and again, the lines among legend and reality become obscured, blocking endeavors to reveal reality. The legend of the lost city of El Dorado is a great representation of how old stories can shape the story and challenge endeavors to find stowed away fortunes.

The progression of time is one more huge obstacle in addressing heists and recuperating treasures. As years transform into long stretches of time, proof might weaken or get derailed, witnesses die, and the path develops cold. In verifiable heist cases, the restricted accessibility of contemporary records and the failure to address living observers present huge hindrances to accomplishing goal. Likewise, the progression of time in the journey for buried fortunes can bring about lost maps, blurred records, and disappearing signs.

The worldwide element of many heist and secret fortune cases adds a layer of intricacy. Hoodlums who commit heists frequently exploit the limits of nations, requiring joint effort among policing, legislatures, and associations around the world. The development of taken resources across worldwide boundaries can thwart endeavors to follow and recuperate them. On account of stowed away fortunes, remote and frequently unknown areas might fall inside the locale of various countries, requiring discretionary collaboration.

One eminent test in the recuperation of taken resources is the presence of a flourishing bootleg market for taken merchandise. Criminal associations and confidential gatherers might hold taken resources, like craftsmanship or gems, for payment or proposition them to purchasers who will address excessive costs. The mystery and intricacy of these exchanges make it hard for policing follow the development of taken resources. The recuperation of taken things frequently requires broad exchanges and lawful instruments to guarantee their re-visitation of their legitimate owners.

On account of stowed away fortunes, the difficulties are similarly overwhelming. Submerged treasures, similar to the freight of the Atocha, might be dispersed across the sea floor, making their recuperation a fastidious and tedious interaction. Archeological fortunes, whether concealed in distant wildernesses or covered underneath antiquated urban areas, request broad exploration, assets, and skill to find and unearth.

In spite of these difficulties, the journey to tackle heists and recuperate stowed away fortunes keeps on enthralling the public's creative mind and rouse the devotion of examiners, travelers, and explorers.

Heists and secret fortunes have enthralled the human creative mind for quite a long time. These captivating stories include the robbery of significant resources and the journey to reveal hid wealth, frequently covered in secret and difficulties. The intentions behind these stories range from monetary benefit and individual enhancement to philosophy and verifiable importance. The cases we have investigated uncover the different idea of these spellbinding stories.

Nervy heists have interested individuals around the world, with crooks executing fastidiously arranged robberies and leaving not many follows. The burglary of the Isabella Stewart Gardner Exhibition hall, the Antwerp Jewel Center heist, and the Lufthansa heist are all demonstration of the craftiness and boldness of heist hoodlums. These cases show the difficulties looked by examiners in following taken resources and securing hoodlums who work in a universe of mystery and misdirection.

Digital heists, like the burglary of cryptographic money from Mt. Gox, show the development of heists in the advanced age. The namelessness and worldwide reach of cybercriminals present remarkable difficulties for policing. Recuperation endeavors in the domain of cybercrime frequently require global participation and high level advanced criminology.

Secret fortunes, then again, frequently include significant resources hid because of reasons going from wartime plundering to old entombment rehearses. The story of the Golden Room and the journey for El Dorado epitomize the appeal of buried treasures. These accounts catch the creative mind and motivate travelers and swashbucklers to set out on journeys into remote and hazardous areas.

The difficulties in tackling heists and it are significant to recuperate stowed away fortunes. The shortage of cement actual proof, the impact of old stories and legends, the progression of time, and the worldwide element of many cases all add layers of intricacy. By and by, the getting through interest with these stories and the commitment of revelation keep on driving the quest for replies.

6.2 The enduring intrigue and potential for future breakthroughs

The persevering through interest encompassing inexplicable problems, heists that stay a secret, and secret fortunes yet to be found is a demonstration of the immortal interest with the obscure and the potential for future forward leaps. These perplexing cases, going from unexplained peculiarities to inexplicable wrongdoings, robberies, and disguised treasures, have caught the public's creative mind for ages. While these secrets present huge difficulties, they likewise rouse interest, decisive reasoning, and a feeling of miracle. This paper investigates the getting through interest of these secrets and the potential for future leap forwards that might disentangle the mysteries they present.

Inexplicable problems have for quite some time been a wellspring of interest, testing how we might interpret the world and the restrictions of human information. The secrets that persevere regardless of broad examinations and the progression of time keep on lighting the creative mind and flash discussion. While some might see perplexing problems as a wellspring of disappointment, they likewise act as a demonstration of the getting through journey for answers and the potential for future revelations.

In the domain of unexplained peculiarities, cases like the presence of cryptids, like the Loch Ness Beast and Bigfoot, have stayed strange for quite a long time. These slippery animals, frequently the subjects of old stories and legend, have caught the public's creative mind, provoking campaigns and examinations looking for definitive proof. The persevering through interest lies in the conviction that there might be something else to the regular world besides science has yet revealed.

The chance of finding obscure species or revealing the insider facts of animals that have long escaped human grasping fills in as a strong inspiration. The improvement of cutting edge innovation, including drones, DNA examination, and remote detecting, offers new roads for exploring these secrets. As how we might interpret environments and the normal world develops, the potential for notable disclosures stays tempting.

Unexplained peculiarities stretch out past cryptids to mysterious occasions like the Tunguska occasion of 1908. The huge blast in Siberia, which smoothed a great many square kilometers of woodland, keeps on confusing researchers and specialists. In spite of broad examinations and various hypotheses, the specific reason for the blast stays unsure. The getting through interest of this occasion is established in the conviction that the response might give significant bits of knowledge into regular peculiarities and planetary dangers.

In the quest for replies to such secrets, the fields of stargazing, geophysics, and ecological science keep on making progressions. Logical leap forwards in fields like meteoritics and environmental science offer expectation that the Tunguska occasion's goal may one day still up in the air. The getting through interest with this secret fills in as a main thrust for additional investigation and comprehension of the universe.

Perplexing vanishings, similar to the secretive evaporating of Malaysia Carriers Flight 370, keep on confusing examiners and the general population. The shortfall of convincing proof with respect to the destiny of the airplane has filled broad ventures and examinations. While the vanishing stays perhaps of the most bewildering case in aeronautics history, it likewise features the potential for headways in innovation and search abilities to reveal insight into such riddles.

In the realm of strange violations, the Dark Dahlia murder and the Zodiac Executioner case are perfect representations of secrets that have persevered for quite a long time. The fierceness of the wrongdoings, enigmatic messages, and tricky culprits have left specialists and general society looking for replies. The getting through interest encompassing these cases has prompted the advancement of new scientific procedures, insightful strategies, and the utilization of current innovation to return to old proof.

Headways in legal science, including DNA examination and criminal profiling, offer new open doors for settling long-cool cases. These forward leaps give trust that the personality of the culprits and the intentions behind the wrongdoings may one day be revealed. The persevering through appeal of these secrets keeps the public drew in and put resources into the mission for equity.

The universe of cybercrime and computerized heists has likewise advanced with the times. Cases like the robbery of cryptographic money from Mt. Gox feature the difficulties presented by the computerized age. While the taken bitcoins esteemed at billions of dollars have never been completely recuperated, the tirelessness of agents and the proceeded with improvement of network safety estimates offer expect relieving such wrongdoings later on.

As innovation propels, so do the techniques utilized by cybercriminals. The continuous wait-and-see game among hoodlums and network safety specialists requires the improvement of state of the art methodologies and devices to safeguard advanced resources. The persevering through interest in these cases comes from the conviction that arrangements might lie in creative methodologies and an extending comprehension of computerized security.

Secret fortunes, whether lost in history or hid in far off areas, keep on being a wellspring of interest. The Golden Room, known as the "Eighth Marvel of the World," stays perhaps of the most pursued treasure ever. In spite of broad endeavors to recuperate the stole from creativity, the Golden Room has escaped disclosure, powering hypothesis and the conviction that it might one day be found.

The difficulties of finding stowed away fortunes, similar to the lost city of El Dorado, frequently spin around verifiable records, legends, and investigation. The headway of remote detecting innovation, satellite imaging, and archeological procedures offers expect revealing these hid wealth. The getting through interest in the mission for buried treasures is the expectation of archeological forward leaps and the potential for uncovering lost human advancements and their significant heritages.

Submerged treasures, similar to the freight of the Spanish ship Nuestra Señora de Atocha, hold the commitment of submerged disclosures. The destruction of the Atocha was situated during the 1980s, bringing about the recuperation of a huge piece of the fortune. Nonetheless, tremendous measures of significant ancient rarities stay unseen on the sea floor, anticipating future submerged investigation and recuperation endeavors.

Headways in marine innovation, including remotely worked vehicles (ROVs) and sonar frameworks, have upgraded the abilities of submerged archeologists and fortune trackers. The persevering through interest with submerged treasures lies in the conviction that state of the art innovation and archeological ability might prompt the recuperation of important verifiable antiques and wealth lost to the profundities of the ocean.

The getting through interest encompassing these inexplicable problems, heists, and secret fortunes isn't just a question of interest yet in addition a demonstration of the unstoppable human soul. It mirrors the unquenchable interest, the journey for replies, and the conviction that, with time and progressions in science, innovation, and analytical strategies, large numbers of these secrets might be unwound.

The potential for future leap forwards is a main impetus behind the persevering through charm of these puzzles. Science and innovation have made critical progressions in ongoing many years, offering new apparatuses and methods for examination and revelation. With the guide of state of the art innovation, DNA examination, remote detecting, and computational calculations, secrets that have long frustrated agents might be near the precarious edge of goal.

In the domain of unexplained peculiarities, the utilization of cutting edge observation frameworks, satellite imaging, and natural checking can possibly yield forward leaps. These apparatuses offer the amazing chance to catch proof of cryptids or surprising regular peculiarities. Furthermore, the ascent of resident science and publicly supported information assortment can grow the range of examinations, giving a more prominent probability of uncovering new data.

Mechanical headways in flying and oceanography can possibly work on the quest for missing airplane and submerged treasures. Complex sonar frameworks and submerged mechanical technology can upgrade remote ocean investigation, offering the chance of finding tragically missing wrecks and their important freight. High level pursuit and salvage methods and satellite imaging can likewise assume a basic part in finding missing airplane.

The improvement of man-made consciousness and AI has changed the universe of scientific science and criminal profiling. These devices can break down tremendous datasets and distinguish examples and associations that might have escaped specialists previously. As innovation keeps on advancing, the potential for addressing cold cases and catching crooks who have dodged catch for quite a long time develops.

In the computerized domain, progressions in network safety measures and the utilization of blockchain innovation can possibly safeguard advanced resources and forestall future digital heists. The continuous cooperation between policing, online protection specialists, and worldwide associations can prompt more successful methodologies for combatting cybercrime and following taken advanced resources.

The journey for buried loves likewise profits by innovative advancement. Remote detecting innovations, like LiDAR (Light Identification and Running) and satellite imaging, empower specialists and archeologists to investigate remote and unavailable areas, uncovering long-covered archeological destinations and the potential for finding disguised wealth. The continuous utilization of ground-entering radar and high level planning apparatuses can upgrade the possibilities finding treasures concealed in the earth.

Moreover, global participation in the field of social legacy safeguarding and bringing home has prompted cooperative endeavors to recuperate taken craftsmanship and authentic antiques. Arrangements and associations devoted to the compensation of social property assume a urgent part in the recuperation of stolen from treasures, encouraging expectation for goal in the years to come.

The getting through charm of perplexing problems, heists, and secret fortunes likewise significantly affects public commitment and instruction. These baffling cases energize decisive reasoning, logical request, and the quest for truth. They move people to seek after vocations in fields like analytical news-casting, policing, science, archaic exploration, and the protection of social legacy.

The getting through interest with these secrets is a demonstration of the human soul of request and the conviction that the obscure can be revealed. It is an update that, even in a world loaded up with complex inquiries and conundrums, the quest for information and truth stays a fundamental human undertaking.

Chapter 7

The Legacy of Heists

The universe of heists, described by bold burglaries and elaborate plans, has made a permanent imprint on history, culture, and society. Heists have propelled interest and interest, enthralling the public's creative mind through accounts of shrewd law-breakers, trying burglaries, and the quest for badly gotten gains. This article investigates the tradition of heists, inspecting their effect on mainstream society, policing, and the persevering through interest with these high-stakes criminal undertakings.

Heists have reliably assumed a noticeable part in molding mainstream society. From exemplary movies to holding books and TV series, the heist type has given perpetual amusement to crowds. Notable heist motion pictures, for example, "Sea's Eleven," "Intensity," and "The Italian Work" have excited watchers with complex plots, essential characters, and amazing activity groupings.

These true to life portrayals frequently feature the mystique of hoodlums and the careful arranging that goes into a fruitful heist. Crowds are attracted to the excitement of the pursuit, the pressure of the wrongdoing, and the fulfillment of a top notch plan. The tradition of heists in mainstream society is the persevering through allure of screw-ups and the appeal of the crook plan.

The impact of heists in mainstream society reaches out past motion pictures. Books like "The Thomas Crown Undertaking" and "The Incomparable Train Burglary" have additionally investigated the universe of heists, digging into the brain research of crooks and the analysts who seek after them. TV series, for example, "Breaking Terrible" and "Cash Heist," have additionally promoted the heist type, depicting the ethical intricacies of criminal ventures.

The tradition of heists in mainstream society is the getting through interest with moral equivocalness, the excitement of intricate plans, and the charm of cunning heroes who obscure the lines among good and bad. These made up depictions have added to the persevering through charm of heists and keep on enthralling crowds around the world.

Heists significantly affect the field of policing security. The difficulties presented by brassy burglaries have prompted headways in safety efforts, analytical strategies, and global participation. Policing have needed to adjust to the developing strategies of lawbreakers, utilizing state of the art innovation and measurable science to battle complex heists.

The tradition of heists in policing the steady quest for development and the drive to remain one stride in front of crooks. The waiting game between law implementation and hoodlums has pushed the limits of analytical techniques, bringing about leap forwards in legal sciences, reconnaissance, and the utilization of witnesses. The continuous journey for equity in heist cases has cultivated cooperation among nearby, public, and worldwide organizations, prompting the worry of famous crooks.

One of the most scandalous heist cases that altogether affected policing the Lufthansa heist at John F. Kennedy Global Air terminal in 1978. The execution of the heist and the tricky idea of the hoodlums tested policing, prompting the advancement of additional refined insightful techniques. The case was instrumental in propelling the utilization of sources, witness security programs, and legal procedures.

The continuous quest for equity in heist cases has likewise brought about the improvement of data sets and data sharing organizations that empower policing to team up on a worldwide scale. These drives have been instrumental in tackling cold cases, following the developments of lawbreakers, and recuperating taken resources.

In the domain of safety, heists have prodded the advancement of imaginative measures to safeguard important resources. Banks, historical centers, and workmanship displays have put resources into cutting edge security frameworks, including observation cameras, access control, and caution frameworks. The transportation of important resources has likewise seen progressions in secure coordinated factors and following innovation.

The tradition of heists in security is the consistent improvement of defensive measures and the obligation to impeding hoodlums' endeavors. The heist classification has featured the weaknesses in security frameworks, provoking organizations and foundations to adjust and improve their protections. This continuous weapons contest among lawbreakers and security experts has added to a more secure and safer climate for significant resources.

Heists have not just influenced mainstream society, policing, security yet have likewise left an enduring heritage in the domain of public discernment and interest. The getting through appeal of heists lies in the strain among reverence and judgment. While heists are criminal demonstrations that frequently include brutality and mischief, they additionally feature the shrewdness and knowledge of the culprits.

The tradition of heists in open discernment is the ethical equivocalness they present. Crowds and people in general are frequently attracted to the moxy and dauntlessness of heist lawbreakers, even as they perceive the culpability of their activities.

This perplexing transaction of feelings mirrors the persevering through interest with screw-ups who challenge the regular limits of good and bad.

Heists have additionally added to the public's interest with the idea of the ideal wrongdoing. The fastidious preparation, complex execution, and the chance of a perfect escape are components that charm the creative mind. The tradition of heists is the continuous investigation of human creativity and the longing to outfox the framework.

The public's interest with heists is additionally filled by the genuine part of these violations. Famous heists like the Incomparable Train Burglary and the Verge's Occupation have turned into the stuff of legends, with their stories of trying adventures and astute crooks. The getting through tradition of heists is the propagation of these accounts, went down through ages as useful examples and wellsprings of motivation.

Heists have not just influenced culture, policing, and public interest however have likewise had monetary outcomes. The burglary of important resources, whether as money, workmanship, or valuable diamonds, can bring about huge monetary misfortunes. Organizations, exhibition halls, and people who succumb to heists might experience monetary difficulties and close to home pain.

The tradition of heists in the monetary circle is the accentuation on risk the executives and protection. Associations that handle significant resources put resources into insurance contracts to alleviate expected misfortunes in case of burglary. These strategies frequently incorporate arrangements for robbery, shortfall, and harm, giving a wellbeing net to the individuals who might succumb to heists.

Insurance agency, thusly, utilize risk appraisal and endorsing practices to decide the degree of inclusion and charges. The evaluation of hazard factors, for example, safety efforts and the verifiable predominance of robbery in a specific region, assumes an essential part in deciding protection rates. The tradition of heists in the monetary area is the continuous refinement of hazard assessment and inclusion to address the advancing strategies of lawbreakers.

The tradition of heists additionally reaches out to the universe of the scholarly community and criminal science. The investigation of heists and their culprits has added to a more profound comprehension of criminal way of behaving and measurable science. Crime analysts and criminal clinicians investigate the inspirations, philosophies, and brain science of heist hoodlums, giving bits of knowledge that illuminate policing and arrangements.

The tradition of heists in scholarly community is the investigation of the crook mind and the improvement of profiles that guide in criminal examinations. The investigation of heists has prompted a more noteworthy comprehension of the inspirations driving such wrongdoings, whether driven by monetary profit, belief system, or a longing for reputation. Crime analysts and criminological specialists keep on leading exploration and distribute discoveries that shed light on the strategies and brain research of heist crooks.

The getting through interest with heists is likewise reflected in the domain of brain research and social science. The charm of heists lies in the adventure of the obscure, the potential for abundance, and the fulfillment of outmaneuvering the specialists. This perplexing interchange of human feelings, including risk-taking, impulsivity, and the longing for acknowledgment, gives important bits of knowledge into the law-breaker mind.

The tradition of heists in brain science is the investigation of the elements that drive people to take part in high-stakes crimes. The investigation of heists has added to how we might interpret criminal way of behaving and the inspirations that underlie these nervy violations. The bits of knowledge acquired from this exploration are pertinent not exclusively to criminal science yet additionally to fields like gamble appraisal, policing, and the avoidance of crimes.

Heists, in their different structures and inspirations, keep on being a subject of interest and interest. Their heritage perseveres in mainstream society, policing, measures, public discernment, financial matters, the scholarly world, and brain science. The getting through appeal of heists is established in the pressure among deference and judgment, the charm of wannabes, and the interest with the idea of the ideal wrongdoing.

While heists address criminal demonstrations with certifiable outcomes, they likewise act as a wellspring of diversion, a concentrate in human way of behaving, and a sign of the getting through interest with bold burglaries and the persevering through quest for equity. The tradition of heists is a demonstration of the persevering through effect of these enthralling stories on our way of life, society, and aggregate creative mind.

7.1 The impact of high-stakes heists on art, culture, and security

High-stakes heists, portrayed by venturesome robberies of important craftsman-ships, valuable jewels, and social relics, have made a permanent imprint on the universe of workmanship, culture, and security. These trying wrongdoings frequently include lawbreakers who carefully plan and execute burglaries from exhibition halls, displays, and confidential assortments, leaving a path of interest and challenge afterward. This exposition investigates the significant effect of high-stakes heists on craftsmanship, culture, and security, looking at the ramifications for these interconnected areas and the persevering through interest they hold.

Workmanship has for quite some time been a vehicle of human articulation and social importance. Historical centers and displays all over the planet house inestimable show-stoppers that not just add to the social legacy of a general public yet additionally act as windows into the past, recounting accounts of innovativeness, history, and the human experience. High-stakes heists focusing on workmanship and social curios significantly affect the universe of imaginative legacy.

Quite possibly of the most famous high-stake craftsmanship heists is the burglary of the Isabella Stewart Gardner Historical center in 1990. Two men dressed as cops entered the gallery in Boston, Massachusetts, and took 13 bits of workmanship esteemed at around $500 million. The taken work of art included magnum opuses by specialists like Vermeer, Rembrandt, and Degas. Notwithstanding broad examinations and endeavors to recuperate the taken pieces, they stay missing, presenting this defense one of the biggest strange craftsmanship heists on the planet.

The effect of high-stakes heists on workmanship is diverse. As a matter of some importance, the robbery of significant craftsmanships addresses a huge misfortune to social legacy. Precious bits of craftsmanship are indispensable, and their nonappearance makes a void in the imaginative and social story. Taken fine arts are lost to the general population as well as become helpless against harm or disregard, further undermining their protection.

The getting through charm of workmanship burglary, as depicted in mainstream society, has additionally energized the tradition of high-stakes heists in the craftsmanship world. Motion pictures like "The Thomas Crown Undertaking" and "The Pink Jaguar" series have depicted the cunning and magnetic craftsmanship hoodlum, catching the creative mind of crowds. The tradition of high-stakes heists in workmanship is the romanticized picture of the craftiness craftsmanship criminal, frequently depicted as a wannabe in movies and writing.

High-stakes workmanship heists have prompted expanded mindfulness and accentuation on craftsmanship security and protection. Historical centers and displays have put resources into cutting edge safety efforts, including observation frameworks, alert frameworks, and access control. Workmanship establishments have additionally supported their staff preparing to

forestall burglary and answer successfully if there should be an occurrence of an episode. The tradition of high-stakes heists in the craftsmanship world is the ceaseless improvement of safety efforts and conventions to defend social fortunes.

The effect of high-stakes heists reaches out to the social area too. Workmanship foundations and exhibitions assume a basic part in safeguarding and advancing social legacy, filling in as overseers of creative and verifiable heritages. The burglary of significant craftsmanships disturbs the social biological system, influencing the capacity of these organizations to satisfy their missions.

The getting through interest encompassing high-stakes heists in the workmanship world is the strain between adoration for the daringness of the wrongdoing and judgment of the crooks who target social fortunes. The media and public frequently end up enamored by the accounts of trying craftsmanship robberies while at the same time grieving the deficiency of indispensable bits of social history.

The tradition of high-stakes heists in culture is the continuous discussion over the morals and ethical quality of workmanship robbery. Questions emerge about the inspirations of lawbreakers who take craftsmanships and the effect of their activities on society's social legacy. This discussion mirrors the mind boggling exchange of interest with daring wrongdoings and the comprehension of the social worth of workmanship.

High-stakes workmanship heists additionally cross with the universe of safety, provoking critical progressions in safety efforts, examination methods, and worldwide collaboration. Security organizations, policing, associations devoted to the recuperation of taken craftsmanship have grown new methodologies to battle workmanship burglary and recuperate taken pieces.

One of the difficulties in tending to high-stakes craftsmanship heists is the global component of many cases. Lawbreakers frequently exploit the limits of nations, getting taken resources across lines to stay away from recognition. The recuperation of taken craftsmanship frequently requires cooperation among policing, state run administrations, and associations around the world. The tradition of high-stakes heists in security is the accentuation on worldwide collaboration and data sharing to follow and capture craftsmanship lawbreakers.

Another huge test is the presence of a flourishing underground market for taken workmanship. Criminal associations might hold important fine arts for payment or offer them to private authorities who will follow through on over the top costs for such fortunes. The mystery and intricacy of these exchanges make it challenging for policing follow the development of taken resources. The recuperation of taken things frequently requires broad talks and lawful systems to guarantee their re-visitation of their original owners.

Progressions in scientific science and innovation have likewise assumed an essential part in tending to high-stakes workmanship heists. The advancement of strategies for the investigation of works of art, including DNA examination, unique mark distinguishing proof, and materials investigation, has worked on the capacity to confirm the validness of recuperated workmanship and indict craftsmanship hoodlums. The tradition of high-stakes heists in security is the persistent headway of criminological procedures that guide in the distinguishing proof and recuperation of taken craftsmanship.

High-stakes heists have prompted the foundation of data sets and data sharing organizations committed to taken craftsmanship. These drives empower policing, exhibition halls, displays, and craftsmanship establishments to team up on a worldwide scale. The advancement of far reaching data sets of taken workmanship and social relics has been instrumental in addressing craftsmanship burglary cases, following the developments of hoodlums, and working with the recuperation of taken resources.

The persevering through interest with high-stakes workmanship heists is established in the double idea of these wrongdoings. They challenge the impression of crooks as simple transgressors, frequently depicting them as clever screw-ups who outmaneuver security frameworks and policing. The tradition of high-stakes workmanship heists in security is the constant quest for advancement and watchfulness to safeguard social fortunes and maintain the uprightness of craftsmanship foundations.

Quite possibly of the most well known high-stake craftsmanship heists is the robbery of "The Shout" by Edvard Crunch from the Public Exhibition in Oslo, Norway, in 1994. The taken composition, perhaps of the most conspicuous and notable craftsmanship on the planet, was recuperated in a sting activity in 1994. The persevering through interest encompassing "The Shout" heist lies in the worldwide acknowledgment of the artistic creation and the boldness of the hoodlums who designated it.

The effect of high-stakes heists on workmanship and culture is apparent in the persevering through interest with these cases. Accounts of craftsmanship robberies, their trying execution, and the boldness of crooks keep on enamoring the public's creative mind. Narratives, books, and media inclusion have additionally sustained the tradition of high-stakes craftsmanship heists, keeping these accounts alive in the social cognizance.

High-stakes craftsmanship heists have likewise prodded the improvement of associations and drives committed to the compensation of taken workmanship and social property. Peaceful accords and associations zeroed in on social legacy protection assume an essential part in tending to workmanship robbery and the recuperation of stolen from treasures. The tradition of high-stakes heists in culture is the obligation to the bringing home of taken craftsmanship and the safeguarding of social legacy.

While high-stakes craftsmanship heists address criminal demonstrations with genuine results, they likewise act as a wellspring of diversion, moral discussion, and motivation. These venturesome robberies challenge the limits of legitimateness and ethical quality, making an imprint on craftsmanship, culture, and security that reaches out past the taken works of art themselves.

7.2 Reflection on the lasting fascination with audacious crimes

The persevering through interest with venturesome wrongdoings, going from heists and craftsmanship robberies to trying breaks and complex secrets, mirrors a multi-layered interchange of human brain research, culture, and cultural elements. These spellbinding stories, both fictitious and genuine, lastingly affect our aggregate creative mind and bring up issues about profound quality, equity, and the limits of human way of behaving. This article investigates the significant and enduring interest with venturesome violations, analyzing the elements that add to our persevering through revenue in these stories.

The appeal of venturesome wrongdoings can be followed back to a portion of the crucial parts of human instinct. Interest, a characteristic profoundly implanted in our mind, frequently drives our advantage in the exceptional and the flighty. Bold wrongdoings are by their very nature exceptional, testing laid out standards and shows. The interest to comprehend the intentions and techniques behind these activities is an essential driver of our interest.

The daringness of these violations is additionally intently attached to our tendency to push limits and look for thrills. Venturesome hoodlums work on the edges of society, frequently opposing the law and cultural standards. Their activities present a feeling of risk and energy that can charm to some. The thought of people ready to face colossal challenges for monetary benefit, reputation, or a feeling of experience takes advantage of the rush looking for part of human brain research.

Besides, the interest with venturesome wrongdoings frequently comes from our reverence of keenness and shrewd. Bold crooks, especially the people who plan and execute heists or elaborate plans, are in many cases depicted as exceptionally canny and fit people. We are attracted to their capacity to outfox specialists, devise complicated designs, and adjust to evolving conditions. This scholarly test, where we attempt to unwind their systems and thought processes, adds to our interest.

Generally speaking, brassy hoodlums are likewise ace controllers, gifted in the specialty of duplicity and confusion. Their capacity to arrange elaborate plans, make redirections, and control insights adds one more layer of interest. We are enraptured by their ability to control and impact the circumstances they think of themselves as in.

Venturesome wrongdoings frequently typify the idea of the wannabe. These are characters who, while perpetrating criminal demonstrations, are depicted with characteristics or conditions that make them engaging or even thoughtful somewhat. This ethical uncertainty challenges regular thoughts of good and bad, and the strain among judgment and esteem turns into a focal subject in a large number of these stories.

The persevering through interest with venturesome wrongdoings isn't restricted to fictitious depictions; it stretches out to genuine cases that definitely stand out enough to be noticed. High-stakes heists, trying jail get away, and strange problems keep on enamoring general society and the media. Genuine daring violations are in many cases set apart by the dauntlessness of the lawbreakers, their capacity to avoid catch, and the persona encompassing their activities.

One of the most famous instances of a genuine bold wrongdoing is the robbery of the Royal gems from the Pinnacle of London in 1671. Thomas Blood, a man with a background marked by crimes, concocted a thinking for even a moment to game plan to take the significant gems. He figured out how to enter the Pinnacle, curb a gate-keeper, and almost prevailed with regards to grabbing the fortune. His daringness and the brassy idea of the wrongdoing had an enduring effect on history.

The effect of bold wrongdoings, whether genuine or fictitious, is additionally clear in their impact on mainstream society. Books, films, TV series, and different types of media have reliably drawn motivation from daring lawbreakers and their capers. Notable fictitious people like Arsène Lupin, Sherlock Holmes, and James Bond are known for their nervy endeavors.

Quite possibly of the most celebrated figure in wrongdoing fiction is Arsène Lupin, made by French essayist Maurice Leblanc. Lupin is a man of honor hoodlum who outsmarts both the police and his lawbreaker rivals with his insight and appeal. The person has turned into an image of bold culpability, interesting to crowds with his mind and daringness.

Additionally, the persevering through notoriety of Sherlock Holmes, made by Sir Arthur Conan Doyle, lays on the splendid investigator's capacity to address venturesome wrongdoings and outmaneuver hoodlums. His rational thinking, sharp perceptions, and venturesome techniques for examination have made him a persevering through figure in writing and film.

The personality of James Bond, as depicted in Ian Fleming's books and a long-running film establishment, typifies the venturesome covert operative who sets out on high-stakes missions. Bond's trying activities, daring plans, and moxy have made him a social symbol and an image of dauntlessness in the realm of undercover work.

Notwithstanding imaginary people, daring genuine lawbreakers have additionally roused books, narratives, and movies. The brassy jail break of Alcatraz escapees Straightforward Morris and the Anglin siblings in 1962, which included a complicated arrangement to escape from perhaps of the most dependable jail in the US, has been the subject of various books and a Clint Eastwood film, "Getaway from Alcatraz."

Genuine hoodlums, for example, the bank looter John Dillinger, the workmanship cheat Isabella Stewart Gardner Gallery criminals, and the nervy slick person Houdini have been depicted in movies and narratives that commend their boldness.

Bold violations likewise track down their direction into different types of workmanship, including visual expressions and music. Compositions, figures, and other creative articulations frequently investigate subjects of daringness and guiltiness. Specialists are attracted to the intricacies and moral ambiguities of nervy wrongdoings, involving them as subjects for their work.

For instance, "Mona Lisa Slipping a Flight of stairs" by Marcel Duchamp, a canvas that consolidates components of Leonardo da Vinci's "Mona Lisa" with the idea of movement and plunge, entertains the concept of workmanship moving and the boldness of rethinking a notable show-stopper. This work difficulties conventional ideas of craftsmanship and boldness in an energetic and provocative way.

In the domain of music, melodies and organizations frequently draw motivation from brassy violations and criminal characters. Bounce Dylan's tune "Storm" recounts the tale of Rubin "Typhoon" Carter, a fighter improperly indicted for homicide. The tune is a strong story that tends to the boldness of the wrongdoing, the unsuccessful labor of equity, and the quest for truth.

The effect of brassy violations on craftsmanship and culture is apparent in the getting through interest with topics of boldness, disobedience, and rebellion. These stories challenge laid out standards, incite thought, and welcome the crowd to investigate the limits of profound quality and human way of behaving. Whether in writing, film, visual expressions, or music, brassy violations keep on giving rich material to imaginative articulation and investigation.

Venturesome violations additionally converge with the universe of equity and policing. The quest for venturesome crooks frequently turns into a high-stakes and constant undertaking, testing the capacities and assets of policing. These lawbreakers, whether depicted in fiction or experienced, in actuality, test the restrictions of the general set of laws and the capacities of those entrusted with catching them.

One of the most notable genuine brassy crooks is D. B. Cooper, who in 1971 seized a business carrier, got a payoff, and dropped out of the plane, vanishing suddenly. The daringness of his activities, alongside his puzzling vanishing, has presented the defense quite possibly of the most persevering through perplexing problem in criminal history.

The effect of daring wrongdoings on policing reflected in the broad assets and examinations devoted to settling these cases. High-stakes heists, daring getaways, and complex secrets frequently require the cooperation of different policing, measurable specialists, and analysts. These cases become practices in critical thinking, procedure, and the utilization of cutting edge scientific strategies.

Bold violations likewise feature the difficulties of ward and worldwide collaboration. Hoodlums who work across borders present extraordinary difficulties for policing. Cases that include the burglary of important workmanship, gemstones, or different resources frequently require the participation of various nations to follow and capture the offenders.

The tradition of venturesome violations in policing the quest for development and cooperation in settling complex cases. The requirement for data sharing, the improvement of measurable innovation, and worldwide collaboration has become progressively significant in tending to nervy wrongdoings that rise above public limits.

The interest with brassy violations is additionally intently attached to their effect on the domains of safety and chance administration. Organizations, foundations, and people frequently end up at the focal point of daring violations, and these encounters shape the manner in which they approach security and chance alleviation.

The effect of bold violations on security is clear in the requirement for cutting edge safety efforts. Organizations, banks, galleries, and different establishments dealing with important resources put resources into state of the art security frameworks to safeguard their properties. These actions frequently incorporate cutting edge observation, access control, alert frameworks, and security work force.

One of the most well known instances of bold lawbreaker arranging is the Lufthansa heist at John F. Kennedy Worldwide Air terminal in 1978. The boldness of the heist and the crooks' capacity to penetrate perhaps of the most reliable air terminal in the US provoked a reassessment of safety efforts in the flight and planned operations businesses.

The tradition of bold violations in security is the nonstop improvement of defensive measures to protect important resources. The difficulties presented by venturesome crooks frequently lead to progressions in security innovation, conventions, and faculty preparing.

Notwithstanding safety efforts, the effect of bold violations is clear in the protection business. The burglary of important resources, whether as workmanship, cash, or valuable jewels, can bring about critical monetary misfortunes. Organizations, galleries, and people frequently go to insurance contracts to alleviate likely misfortunes in case of robbery or misfortune.

The tradition of bold wrongdoings in the protection area is the accentuation on risk evaluation and guaranteeing. Insurance agency utilize risk evaluation practices to decide the degree of inclusion and expenses. These evaluations consider factors, for example, safety efforts, the verifiable commonness of burglary in a specific region, and the particular dangers related with the resources being protected.

The persevering through interest with venturesome violations isn't restricted to the adventure of the actual wrongdoing yet reaches out to the quest for equity and the goal of these intricate cases. The general population, media, and policing frequently become profoundly engaged with the endeavors to tackle brassy violations, making these cases a focal point of consideration and conversation.

One of the most getting through strange problems is the vanishing of Malaysia Carriers Flight 370 of every 2014. The venturesome idea of the episode, which included the evaporating of a business carrier with 239 individuals ready, has prompted broad examinations and searches. The continuous mission to decide the destiny of the airplane and its travelers mirrors the getting through interest with bold secrets.

Bold wrongdoings frequently catch the public's creative mind, inciting conversations, discussions, and examinations that reach out for a really long time, or even many years. These cases challenge the crowd to think basically, investigate alternate points of view, and consider the different variables that add to their getting through interest.

The persevering through appeal of venturesome violations is additionally reflected in the domain of brain research and conduct science. The inspirations, brain science, and conduct of venturesome crooks act as subjects of study and exploration. Clinicians, crime analysts, and scientific specialists try to comprehend what drives people to take part in high-stakes and brassy crimes.

The tradition of brassy wrongdoings in brain science is the investigation of the elements that underlie risk-taking way of behaving, impulsivity, and the longing for acknowledgment. These investigations shed light on the intricate interchange of human feelings and inspirations, adding to how we might interpret criminal way of behaving.

Besides, the interest with venturesome violations frequently reaches out to the domain of public insight and social effect. Nervy lawbreakers, both fictitious and genuine, can become famous figures, representing dauntlessness, disobedience, and insubordination. Their accounts challenge traditional ideas of gallantry and villainy, welcoming us to scrutinize the limits of good and bad.

The getting through charm of nervy wrongdoings is additionally established in the idea of the ideal wrongdoing. The careful preparation, multifaceted execution, and the chance of an impeccable escape are components that spellbind the creative mind. These accounts challenge how we might interpret human resourcefulness and the longing to outmaneuver the framework.

Chapter 8

Modern Heists and the Future

Current heists, described by refined strategies, computerized development, and the steadily developing scene of culpability, present an imposing test to policing security organizations all over the planet. These venturesome violations incorporate a great many exercises, including digital heists, cryptographic money robbery, craftsmanship and curio burglary, and high-stakes thefts. This article dives into the universe of present day heists, looking at the developing techniques and their effect on society, as well as the systems and advancements that might shape the eventual fate of battling such wrongdoings.

The computerized unrest has not just changed the manner in which we live and work yet has likewise given new roads to crooks to execute heists on a worldwide scale. Digital heists, specifically, have turned into a huge danger to people, organizations, and legislatures. These wrongdoings include the burglary of advanced resources, like delicate data, monetary information, and licensed innovation.

One of the most notorious digital heists in late history is the 2014 assault on Sony Pictures. Programmers, purportedly supported by North Korea, penetrated the's organization, took delicate data, and delivered it to general society. The assault was an unmistakable exhibit of how computerized foes could think twice about large company's security, prompting boundless harm to its standing and tasks.

The effect of digital heists on the cutting edge world is extensive. Past monetary misfortunes, they can possibly think twice about security, dissolve trust in advanced frameworks, and disturb basic foundation. The refinement of cybercriminals, their capacity to take advantage of weaknesses, and the consistently developing nature of innovation make it moving for people and associations to actually safeguard themselves.

Present day heists stretch out past the computerized domain, with lawbreakers utilizing progressed methods to target actual resources also. Craftsmanship and relic burglary, for example, stays a high-stakes try for criminal associations. These heists include the burglary of significant craftsmanships, verifiable ancient rarities, and social fortunes, which frequently have critical social and authentic significance.

The 2010 robbery of two works of art by Vincent van Gogh, "Perspective on the Ocean at Scheveningen" and "Gathering Leaving the Improved Church in Nuenen," from the Van Gogh Gallery in Amsterdam fills in to act as an illustration of the dauntlessness and meaning of workmanship burglary. These taken works of art, esteemed at a huge number of dollars, address an essential region of the planet social legacy, making their burglary a monetary misfortune as well as a disaster for our common history and imaginative heritage.

The effect of workmanship and ancient rarity robbery on culture and legacy conservation is significant. Taken treasures are lost to general society as well as become powerless against harm or disregard, further undermining their conservation. Exhibition halls, displays, and workmanship organizations face the continuous test of offsetting openness with security, trying to safeguard their assortments while imparting them to the world.

Workmanship robbery likewise crosses with the universe of coordinated wrongdoing. Criminal associations might involve taken works of art as a type of cash, a method for laundering cash, or influence for exchange. The bootleg market for taken workmanship is a flourishing industry, frequently covered in mystery and intricacy. Taken craftsmanship can change hands on different occasions, making it hard for policing track and recuperate these significant resources.

High-stakes heists keep on enthralling the public's creative mind through accounts of sly hoodlums, trying burglaries, and the quest for badly gotten gains. These stories challenge how we might interpret the world and the constraints of human information. While these secrets present huge difficulties, they likewise rouse interest, decisive reasoning, and a feeling of miracle. With headways in science, innovation, and analytical strategies, the potential for unwinding these puzzles stays a strong inspiration, cultivating trust for goal and disclosure in the years to come.

One more aspect of present day heists is the robbery of cryptographic money. As computerized monetary standards like Bitcoin and Ethereum have acquired prevalence, they have become rewarding focuses for cybercriminals. Cryptographic money heists include the burglary of computerized resources from online wallets, trades, and stages. Hoodlums utilize different procedures, including hacking, phishing, and ransomware assaults, to think twice about security of these advanced resources.

One of the main cryptographic money heists happened in 2014 when the Mt. Gox trade, which was one of the biggest Bitcoin trades at that point, sought financial protection subsequent to losing roughly 850,000 Bitcoins, esteemed at more than $450 million at that point. The episode featured the weakness of cryptographic money stages to cyberattacks and raised worries about the security of computerized resources.

The effect of digital currency heists isn't restricted to monetary misfortunes. They likewise sabotage trust in computerized monetary standards and blockchain innovation. The capacity of cybercriminals to think twice about security of computerized resources has expansive ramifications for the reception of digital currencies in standard money and business.

The ascent of cryptographic money heists has provoked expanded endeavors to upgrade the security of advanced wallets and trades. Cryptographic money organizations are putting resources into cutting edge safety efforts, for example, multifaceted verification, encryption, and cold stockpiling arrangements, to shield advanced resources from robbery. Moreover, administrative specialists are attempting to lay out systems for the completely safe utilization of digital currencies.

The universe of current heists isn't bound to the domains of cybercrime, craftsmanship robbery, and digital money heists; it likewise incorporates high-stakes actual burglaries. These brassy violations include the burglary of important resources, like money, adornments, or valuable pearls, frequently in trying and whimsical ways.

One such brassy burglary occurred in 2015 when a pack of cheats dug a passage from a leased structure to the vault of the Hatton Nursery Safe Store Organization in London. Over the Easter weekend, they utilized the passage to get to the vault and took a huge number of dollars of money, gems, and different resources. The daringness and fastidious preparation of the heist caught the world's consideration.

The effect of high-stakes actual burglaries is twofold. On one hand, these violations address a critical monetary misfortune to the people in question, who might be people, organizations, or monetary foundations. Then again, they challenge our view of safety and the actions set up to safeguard important resources. These heists highlight the requirement for cutting edge security conventions and careful gamble the board.

High-stakes actual burglaries frequently include arrangement ahead of time, the utilization of innovation, and a profound comprehension of safety frameworks. Hoodlums utilize strategies like penetrating passages, handicapping cautions, or utilizing diversionary techniques to get to their objectives. The dauntlessness of their activities frequently leaves policing confronting complex examinations and critical difficulties.

The effect of present day heists, whether they include cybercrime, cryptographic money robbery, workmanship and antique burglary, or high-stakes actual burglaries, is significant and expansive. These violations challenge how we might interpret security, the limits of guiltiness, and the steadily advancing scene of wrongdoing in the computerized age.

The developing idea of heists represents a considerable test to policing security organizations, requesting advancement in analytical procedures, the utilization of cutting edge innovation, and global participation. The quest for equity in heist cases, whether in the advanced or actual domain, requires broad joint effort among nearby, public, and global offices.

In the computerized domain, progressions in network safety measures and the utilization of blockchain innovation can possibly safeguard advanced resources from digital heists. Blockchain, with its decentralized and unchanging record, offers a promising answer for upgrading the security of digital money exchanges and capacity.

Moreover, policing are progressively zeroing in on computerized criminology to examine cybercrimes and follow the developments of taken advanced resources. The improvement of cutting edge criminological methods for dissecting advanced proof, for example, malware examination, network criminology, and blockchain investigation, is essential in addressing digital heists.

The future of combatting craftsmanship and ancient rarity robbery likewise holds guarantee, with the utilization of cutting edge innovation for following and recuperating taken things. Computerized information bases and organizations devoted to taken craftsmanship empower policing, exhibition halls, displays, and workmanship foundations to team up on a worldwide scale. These data sets are instrumental in addressing craftsmanship robbery cases, following the developments of crooks, and working with the recuperation of taken resources.

Workmanship organizations are additionally embracing creative safety efforts, including best in class observation frameworks, access control, and caution frameworks. The utilization of man-made reasoning (artificial intelligence) and AI in security frameworks considers continuous danger identification and reaction, improving the assurance of important works of art and social antiques.

Cryptographic money heists represent a novel test, yet progressions in blockchain innovation and the advancement of safer computerized wallets and trades are supposed to work on the wellbeing of computerized resources. Administrative specialists are attempting to lay out thorough rules for the utilization of digital currencies, with an emphasis on forestalling and relieving cybercrimes.

In the domain of high-stakes actual burglaries, the future might see the combination of cutting edge security innovation and constant observing to safeguard resources. Biometric access control, savvy sensors, and reconnaissance frameworks are turning out to be more modern, offering upgraded assurance against nervy heists. AI calculations can examine designs and recognize potential security breaks, giving convenient alarms to security faculty.

The getting through interest with nervy wrongdoings isn't just established in that frame of mind of the actual wrongdoing yet in addition chasing after equity and goal. The perplexing idea of these wrongdoings provokes policing to foster inventive procedures, team up across lines, and utilize state of the art innovation to capture lawbreakers and recuperate taken resources.

The universe of current heists, set apart by computerized advancement and developing criminal strategies, is dynamic and always showing signs of change. Crooks persistently adjust to new safety efforts and take advantage of weaknesses in the advanced scene. The future of battling these wrongdoings lies in the proactive utilization of innovation, data sharing, and global participation.

Additionally, the getting through interest with venturesome wrongdoings and the perplexing problems they present keeps on spurring specialists, analysts, and general society. These cases challenge the limits of human information and the restrictions of innovation. The quest for goal in high-stakes heists isn't just a journey for equity yet additionally an investigation of the complicated exchange of brain research, criminal way of behaving, and the developing scene of guiltiness.

In the advanced age, the world is more associated than any other time, considering expanded data dividing and joint effort between policing. Global collaboration is essential in tending to wrongdoings that rise above public limits, for example, digital heists and the burglary of workmanship and ancient rarities.

The utilization of cutting edge innovation, including blockchain, computerized legal sciences, and artificial intelligence, can possibly upset the examination and anticipation of present day heists. These apparatuses offer imaginative ways of getting computerized resources, follow the development of taken property, and break down advanced proof to secure crooks.

While the difficulties presented by venturesome violations are huge, the getting through interest with these cases mirrors the strain between adoration for the dauntlessness of the lawbreakers and the quest for equity. The appeal of brassy wrongdoings keeps on enrapturing our creative mind, motivating decisive reasoning, advancement, and the mission for goal in these complicated secrets.

8.1 A look at contemporary high-stakes heists and trends

Contemporary high-stakes heists keep on catching the world's creative mind, driven by a blend of trying hoodlums, developing innovation, and the charm of tremendous prizes. These brassy wrongdoings length different areas, including digital heists, workmanship and antique robbery, cryptographic money burglary, and elaborate thefts. This exposition gives a top to bottom investigation of contemporary high-stakes heists and the arising patterns that shape the scene of daring crimes.

The computerized age has led to another variety of hoodlums who influence innovation and complexity to coordinate high-stakes heists. Among the most conspicuous of these are digital heists, which include the robbery of advanced resources, touchy data, and licensed innovation. Cybercriminals frequently exploit weaknesses in advanced frameworks to access and take important information.

One of the most notorious digital heists in late memory is the break of Equifax in 2017, where programmers got to the individual data of 143 million Americans. This break featured the dauntlessness and effect of cybercriminals, who can think twice about information on an exceptional scale.

The effect of digital heists on contemporary society is critical. Past the monetary misfortunes caused, they can think twice about security, disintegrate trust in computerized frameworks, and upset basic foundation. The complexity of cybercriminals, their capacity to take advantage of weaknesses, and the quickly advancing innovation scene make it trying for people, organizations, and legislatures to successfully protect computerized resources.

Current heists additionally reach out into the domain of cryptographic money robbery. As advanced monetary standards like Bitcoin and Ethereum have acquired notoriety, they have become rewarding focuses for cybercriminals. Cryptographic money heists include the burglary of computerized resources from online wallets, trades, and stages. Lawbreakers utilize different procedures, including hacking, phishing, and ransomware assaults, to think twice about security of these computerized resources.

One of the main cryptographic money heists happened in 2014 when the Mt. Gox trade, one of the biggest Bitcoin trades at that point, petitioned for financial protection subsequent to losing around 850,000 Bitcoins, esteemed at more than $450 million. The episode featured the weakness of cryptographic money stages to cyberattacks and raised worries about the security of computerized resources.

The effect of digital currency heists isn't restricted to monetary misfortunes. They likewise subvert trust in computerized monetary standards and blockchain innovation. The capacity of cybercriminals to think twice about security of computerized resources has extensive ramifications for the reception of digital currencies in standard money and business.

The universe of contemporary high-stakes heists isn't restricted to the domains of cybercrime and cryptographic money burglary; it additionally envelops high-stakes actual burglaries. These brassy violations include the burglary of significant resources, like money, adornments, or valuable pearls, frequently in trying and eccentric ways.

Quite possibly of the most trying actual heist happened in 2015 when a pack of criminals dug a passage from a leased structure to the vault of the Hatton Nursery Safe Store Organization in London. Over the Easter weekend, they utilized the passage to get to the vault and took a huge number of dollars of money, gems, and different resources. The dauntlessness and fastidious preparation of the heist caught the world's consideration.

The effect of high-stakes actual burglaries is twofold. On one hand, these violations address a critical monetary misfortune to the people in question, who might be people, organizations, or monetary foundations. Then again, they challenge our view of safety and the actions set up to safeguard important resources. These heists highlight the requirement for cutting edge security conventions and watchful gamble the board.

The effect of craftsmanship and curio robbery on contemporary culture and legacy safeguarding is significant. Taken treasures are lost to general society as well as become helpless against harm or disregard, further undermining their safeguarding. Exhibition halls, displays, and craftsmanship organizations face the continuous test of offsetting openness with security, looking to safeguard their assortments while imparting them to the world.

Workmanship burglary likewise meets with the universe of coordinated wrong-doing. Criminal associations might involve taken works of art as a type of cash, a method for laundering cash, or influence for discussion. The bootleg market for taken workmanship is a flourishing industry, frequently covered in mystery and intricacy. Taken craftsmanship can change hands on numerous occasions, making it challenging for policing track and recuperate these significant resources.

High-stakes heists in the workmanship world are set apart by the dauntlessness of the hoodlums, their capacity to dodge catch, and the persona encompassing their activities. The effect of these heists on contemporary culture is clear in the getting through interest with accounts of clever lawbreakers, trying burglaries, and the quest for badly gotten gains. Narratives, books, and media inclusion propagate the tradition of high-stakes workmanship heists, keeping these accounts alive in the social awareness.

The effect of contemporary high-stakes heists on workmanship and culture is extensive. These wrongdoings challenge the impression of workmanship as a static and safeguarded substance, featuring the requirement for upgraded safety efforts and creative conservation methods. The persevering through charm of workmanship robbery, as depicted in mainstream society, has likewise powered the tradition of high-stakes heists in the craftsmanship world. Films like "The Thomas Crown Issue" and "The Pink Puma" series have depicted the astute and magnetic craftsmanship criminal, catching the creative mind of crowds.

High-stakes heists have prompted expanded mindfulness and accentuation on workmanship security and safeguarding. Exhibition halls and displays have put resources into cutting edge safety efforts, including observation frameworks, alert frameworks, and access control. Craftsmanship foundations have likewise reinforced their staff preparing to forestall robbery and answer successfully if there should arise an occurrence of an episode.

Headways in scientific science and innovation have likewise assumed a vital part in tending to high-stakes craftsmanship heists. The advancement of techniques for the investigation of works of art, including DNA examination, unique mark recognizable proof, and substance examination, has worked on the possibilities recuperating taken workmanship. These devices have become fundamental in demonstrating the provenance of works of art and distinguishing taken things.

The universe of high-stakes heists converges with the steadily advancing domain of innovation, introducing the two valuable open doors and difficulties for hoodlums and policing. The advanced age has brought about new techniques for coordinating high-stakes heists, with crooks taking advantage of innovation and the secrecy it gives.

Quite possibly of the main pattern in contemporary high-stakes heists is the utilization of advanced development to target computerized resources and information. Digital heists include the robbery of touchy data, monetary information, and licensed innovation, frequently for a gigantic scope. Hoodlums utilize procedures, for example, hacking, ransomware assaults, and phishing to think twice about frameworks and get close enough to important information.

Digital heists have advanced with the extension of innovation, with lawbreakers persistently looking for new weaknesses to take advantage of. The utilization of cutting edge malware, including ransomware that encodes information until a payment is paid, has turned into a pervasive strategy for assault. This pattern has raised worries about the weakness of basic foundation, government organizations, and confidential partnerships.

The effect of digital heists reaches out to public safety, as aggressors might target government organizations and basic framework. The split the difference of touchy data can have expansive outcomes, including undercover work, blackmail, and the disturbance of fundamental administrations. The pervasiveness of digital heists has provoked legislatures and associations to put resources into cutting edge network safety measures, including danger recognition, occurrence reaction, and data sharing.

One more unmistakable pattern in high-stakes heists is the focusing of cryptographic forms of money. As computerized monetary standards like Bitcoin and Ethereum gain prevalence, they have become worthwhile focuses for cybercriminals. Cryptographic money heists include the burglary of computerized resources from online wallets, trades, and stages. Lawbreakers use procedures, for example, hacking, phishing, and ransomware assaults to think twice about security of these computerized resources.

Cryptographic money heists have become more refined, with lawbreakers taking advantage of the namelessness of computerized monetary forms to launder taken reserves. The ascent of decentralized finance (DeFi) stages has additionally presented new weaknesses, as programmers track down ways of taking advantage of savvy contracts and decentralized applications (dApps).

The effect of digital currency heists stretches out past monetary misfortunes. They can subvert trust in advanced monetary standards and blockchain innovation, easing back their reception in standard money and trade. Administrative specialists are attempting to lay out exhaustive rules for the utilization of digital currencies, with an emphasis on forestalling and relieving cybercrimes.

In the domain of actual high-stakes heists, crooks keep on utilizing imaginative techniques to target important resources. The utilization of diversionary strategies, for example, making interruptions or controlling security faculty, stays a pervasive pattern. Crooks additionally influence their insight into security frameworks and weaknesses to get to their objectives.

One more pattern in high-stakes actual burglaries is the utilization of innovation to design and execute heists. Lawbreakers might utilize drones for observation, specialized gadgets to organize their activities, and, surprisingly, 3D printing to make copies of significant resources.

These advancements challenge policing to adjust and involve innovation for more powerful safety efforts and examination.

Workmanship and relic robbery have likewise seen striking patterns, with hoodlums focusing on unambiguous things of high worth and social importance. The robbery of craftsmanship by notable specialists or verifiable antiquities with one of a kind provenance has become more normal. Lawbreakers might look to hold these things for recover, offer them to private gatherers, or influence them for reputation.

Workmanship burglary meets with the universe of coordinated wrongdoing, as taken fine arts can be utilized as a type of cash for illegal exercises. The bootleg market for taken craftsmanship keeps on flourishing, driven by the interest for important and socially critical things. Craftsmanship foundations and policing are ceaselessly looking for ways of recuperating taken workmanship and safeguard social legacy.

Headways in innovation and scientific science have added to patterns in tending to high-stakes heists. The utilization of computerized information bases and organizations committed to taken workmanship empowers policing, historical centers, exhibitions, and craftsmanship foundations to team up on a worldwide scale. These data sets are instrumental in tackling workmanship burglary cases, following the developments of lawbreakers, and working with the recuperation of taken resources.

The advancement of strategies for the investigation of craftsmanships, including DNA examination, unique mark recognizable proof, and substance investigation, has worked on the possibilities recuperating taken workmanship. These devices have become fundamental in demonstrating the provenance of fine arts and recognizing taken things.

Notwithstanding mechanical headways, the utilization of man-made reasoning (man-made intelligence) and AI plays had an essential impact in upgrading safety efforts. Simulated intelligence controlled observation frameworks can dissect designs, identify abnormalities, and give ongoing danger location. AI calculations can distinguish potential security breaks and give convenient cautions to security staff.

The persevering through charm of high-stakes heists isn't just established in that frame of mind of the actual wrongdoing yet in addition chasing after equity and goal. These complicated cases challenge policing to foster imaginative techniques, team up across lines, and utilize state of the art innovation to catch crooks and recuperate taken resources.

The universe of contemporary high-stakes heists, set apart by computerized advancement and developing criminal strategies, is dynamic and steadily evolving. Hoodlums persistently adjust to new safety efforts and take advantage of weaknesses in the advanced scene. The future of battling these wrongdoings lies in the proactive utilization of innovation, worldwide participation, and creative analytical strategies, driven by the persevering through interest with daring violations and the journey for goal.

8.2 Predictions for the future of treasure heists and law enforcement

Expectations for the eventual fate of fortune heists and policing to battle them are molded by a mix of developing innovations, arising criminal strategies, and the worldwide scene of safety and policing. This exposition dives into possible patterns and advancements in the domain of fortune heists and the methodologies that policing might utilize to address these bold wrongdoings.

Perhaps of the most conspicuous pattern coming soon for treasure heists is the rising intermingling of physical and advanced components. Crooks are probably going to use the furthest down the line innovation to design and execute their heists. Specifically, the utilization of robots for observation and surveillance might turn out to be more predominant. Hoodlums could send robots to survey the security of target areas, assemble data, and screen policing.

The combination of man-made reasoning (artificial intelligence) and AI into security frameworks and reconnaissance cameras will empower continuous danger discovery and examination. Artificial intelligence controlled frameworks can distinguish uncommon examples, perceive expected dangers, and ready security work force. This innovation won't just upgrade the insurance of fortunes yet in addition facilitate policing.

Lawbreakers may likewise utilize 3D printing innovation to make reproductions of important resources. These reproductions can be utilized to confound policing, time for the lawbreakers, or act as payoff influence. The capacity to deliver persuading copies regarding treasures represents a test to verification and recuperation endeavors.

In the advanced domain, digital heists focusing on significant computerized resources and data will keep on developing. Hoodlums might utilize progressed malware and ransomware assaults to think twice about frameworks and get to delicate information. The utilization of digital money for recover installments may likewise turn out to be more normal, as it gives a degree of obscurity that crooks view as engaging.

As the web of things (IoT) extends, there is a potential for crooks to take advantage of weaknesses in associated gadgets. Shrewd security frameworks, like cameras, alerts, and access control, might be designated to work with actual heists or gain unapproved section to got areas.

The eventual fate of fortune heists is additionally impacted by the worldwide scene of coordinated wrongdoing. Criminal organizations might enhance their exercises to incorporate fortune heists for the purpose of laundering cash and securing important resources. The underground market for taken treasures is supposed to flourish, with expanded request from private gatherers and criminal associations trying to take advantage of social ancient rarities and craftsmanship.

Ecological elements and catastrophic events are one more thought for the fate of fortune heists. Rising ocean levels, outrageous climate occasions, and land changes might uncover recently covered up fortunes or curios. Crooks might take advantage of these potential chances to unearth and sneak important things unlawfully.

One expectation for the eventual fate of fortune heists is an expanded spotlight on social relics and authentic fortunes. Lawbreakers may explicitly target things of exceptional provenance, authentic importance, or social significance. The robbery of such fortunes can bring about a huge monetary bonus for crooks, who might hold them for payment or sell them on the bootleg market.

To address these arising patterns in treasure heists, policing should take on creative systems and advancements. One such technique is global collaboration. Treasure heists frequently include the development of taken things across borders, making it fundamental for policing to team up with their worldwide partners. Data sharing, joint examinations, and facilitated endeavors will be vital in capturing hoodlums and recuperating taken treasures.

The utilization of blockchain innovation is supposed to assume a huge part coming down the line for treasure heist examinations. Blockchain's decentralized and unchanging record can be utilized to confirm the genuineness and provenance of fortunes. Relics and important things can be enlisted on a blockchain, giving a protected and straightforward record of proprietorship and history. This innovation can help policing distinguishing taken things and working with their re-visitation of their original owners.

Man-made reasoning and AI will become important devices in treasure heist examinations. These advances can examine immense measures of information, distinguish examples, and help with following the developments of lawbreakers. Computer based intelligence controlled facial acknowledgment frameworks can support the distinguishing proof of suspects, while AI calculations can foresee potential future heist targets in light of authentic information.

Criminological science will keep on advancing, offering new methods for dissecting taken treasures. DNA examination, finger impression distinguishing proof, and synthetic examination will turn out to be more modern, helping with the verification and recuperation of taken things.

Policing should put resources into best in class measurable labs and preparing for their faculty to stay up with these headways.

Also, the fate of fortune heist examinations might include the utilization of quantum registering. Quantum PCs can possibly perform complex estimations at speeds that outperform old style PCs. This capacity can help policing in decoding encoded correspondences and breaking complex codes utilized by crooks.

Prescient policing, driven by information examination and AI, will likewise assume a critical part coming soon for treasure heist counteraction. Policing can utilize verifiable information and examples to anticipate potential heist targets, empowering them to designate assets proactively and upgrade security at weak areas.

The utilization of expanded reality (AR) and computer generated reality (VR) innovation is supposed to support policing and reenactments. Officials can utilize AR and VR to work on answering fortune heist situations, working on their readiness and adequacy, in actuality, circumstances.

Worldwide data sets and organizations committed to taken workmanship and social antiques will proceed to grow and get to the next level. These stages empower policing, historical centers, exhibitions, and craftsmanship establishments to team up on a worldwide scale. Such data sets are instrumental in tackling craftsmanship robbery cases, following the developments of crooks, and working with the recuperation of taken resources.

In the computerized domain, policing should adjust to developing innovation patterns. This incorporates upgrading network safety measures to safeguard computerized resources and delicate data. Normal weakness evaluations, danger discovery, and occurrence reaction plans will be fundamental for shield against digital heists.

Besides, administrative specialists will assume a crucial part in tending to digital money heists. The advancement of extensive rules for the utilization of digital currencies and decentralized finance (DeFi) stages is fundamental for forestalling and alleviating cybercrimes. This guideline will zero in on improving safety efforts, leading exhaustive record verifications on cryptographic money specialist co-ops, and checking exchanges for dubious exercises.

The utilization of advanced legal sciences and blockchain examination will become norm in exploring digital money heists. These devices permit policing to follow the development of taken advanced resources and recognize the people behind the crimes. Fostering the abilities and skill expected to direct powerful computerized criminology will be really important for policing.

In the domain of high-stakes actual heists, safety efforts should adjust to arising patterns in innovation and criminal strategies. The coordination of computer based intelligence controlled observation frameworks, facial acknowledgment innovation, and AI calculations will upgrade continuous danger identification and reaction. These frameworks will turn out to be more modern in distinguishing potential security breaks and cautioning security work force.

The utilization of biometric access control and brilliant sensors will help with getting important resources and areas. These actions give an additional layer of insurance, guaranteeing that main approved people can get to fortunes and relics. The mix of brilliant innovation into security frameworks will turn out to be more pervasive to shield against actual heists.

The utilization of robots in heist situations will provoke policing to foster counter-drone innovation and techniques. Identifying and impairing unapproved robots will be fundamental in keeping lawbreakers from involving them for observation and surveillance. Policing may utilize robots of their own for reconnaissance and fast reaction to heist circumstances.

In case of cataclysmic events and ecological changes, policing and social conservation associations should work together on safeguarding uncovered fortunes and curios. This includes the advancement of crisis reaction plans, secure storage spaces, and methodologies for alleviating the plundering and unlawful exchange of important things.

Preparing and readiness will be key parts of policing to address arising patterns in treasure heists. Staff should remain refreshed on the most recent innovation, scientific strategies, and insightful techniques. Normal activities and recreations that imitate heist situations will assist policing with planning for genuine circumstances.

The fate of fortune heists and policing to battle them will be formed by a perplexing transaction of innovation, criminal inventiveness, and worldwide collaboration. As hoodlums keep on adjusting to new safety efforts, policing should remain ahead by embracing development, cooperation, and the utilization of state of the art innovation.

Chapter 9

Conclusion

In this awe-inspiring excursion through the records of history, we have set out on an elating experience, disclosing the spellbinding universe of fortune heists. "Narratives of Wealth" has taken us on a hypnotizing odyssey crossing hundreds of years and mainlands, uncovering stories of boldness, sly, and interest. As we finish up our investigation of these enthralling stories, we wind up at a junction where the at various times blend, making a clear embroidery of human desire, constancy, and, on occasion, offense.

The charm of fortune has been a steady power all through mankind's set of experiences. It rises above topographical limits and social contrasts, joining individuals in their quest for abundance, power, and the fortunes that guarantee both. Our process started with an investigation of the earliest realized treasure heists, diving into the adventures of the finesse thieves who tried to gain wealth from old burial places and sanctuaries. These accounts portrayed the lengths to which people were ready to go as they continued looking for gold, diamonds, and valuable relics. The tradition of these early fortune heists is a persevering through demonstration of the human interest with abundance and the persevering through want to have it, even at incredible gamble.

As we wandered further into the archives of history, we experienced accounts of privateers, marauders, and daring explorers who pillaged huge fortunes on the high oceans. The stories of privateers like Blackbeard, Chief Kidd, and Anne Bonny spellbound our minds, exhibiting the trying endeavors and misleading existences of the individuals who picked an existence of sea robbery. Their merciless quest for treasure on the vast sea exhibited the lengths to which people would go to store up riches, regardless of whether it implied living a dangerous presence loaded up with savagery and vulnerability.

Pushing ahead, we dove into the universe of terrific heists and trying tricks, where venturesome cheats utilized clever techniques to outmaneuver specialists and take precious fortunes. The scandalous robbery of the Mona Lisa by Vincenzo Peruggia and the nervy adventures of the Pink Puma Pack exemplified the inventiveness and boldness of the individuals who sought to free significant fine arts from the bounds of historical centers and exhibitions. These accounts exhibited the intricate interchange of workmanship, wrongdoing, and the overpowering charm of high-stakes burglary.

Our process additionally took us through the pages of history where people, driven by eagerness and aspiration, serious venturesome heists in the domain of coordinated wrongdoing. The endeavors of criminal geniuses like John Dillinger and the Incomparable Train Burglary pack exhibited the perplexing preparation and execution expected to coordinate heists of such scale and boldness. These accounts revealed the hazier side of human instinct, where the journey for abundance could prompt disorder and brutality.

In the cutting edge time, the world saw the introduction of another variety of fortune trackers and globe-trotters. The narratives of remote ocean adventurers, for example, Mel Fisher, who committed their lives to uncovering the wealth lost underneath the sea's profundities, uncovered the steadiness and assurance expected to uncover treasures concealed by time and the components. The story of the rescue of the Atocha's tremendous wealth offered a convincing investigate the crash of history, innovation, and desire in the journey for submerged fortune.

"Accounts of Wealth" additionally carried us eye to eye with the baffling universe of social bringing home and the dubious morals encompassing the arrival of taken relics and fortunes to their nations of beginning. The bringing home of the Elgin Marbles and the Benin Bronzes shed light on the mind boggling discusses encompassing the legitimate responsibility for legacy and the ethical basic to reestablish fortunes to their places of beginning. These accounts uncovered the perplexing trap of legislative issues, morals, and history that encompass the universe of taken treasures.

All through our excursion, we experienced a common subject of the persevering through charm of fortune and the lengths to which people and social orders will go in quest for wealth. The tales of fortune heists disclosed a significant human interest with riches, influence, and the fortunes that represent them. An interest rises above general setting, a widespread desire that has formed the course of history.

In our investigation of these charming stories, we likewise noticed the diverse effect of fortune heists on people, networks, and countries. While certain heists prompted fortune and greatness for the culprits, they frequently abandoned a path of obliteration, fights in court, and moral difficulties. The results of fortune heists reached out past the prompt demonstration of robbery, influencing the social and verifiable accounts of the spots from which fortunes were taken and the destinies of those included.

"Narratives of Wealth" further featured the always advancing endeavors to safeguard and save treasures. The foundation of historical centers, secure vaults, and high level safety efforts addresses a huge reaction to the continuous danger of burglary. The story of the Isabella Stewart Gardner Historical center heist and the ensuing endeavors to recuperate the taken fine arts highlighted the responsibility of organizations and policing to protect our common social legacy.

Our process additionally divulged the energetic work of people, researchers, and activists who have committed their lives to the recuperation and safeguarding of taken treasures. Their faithful assurance and devotion despite difficulty act as a demonstration of the human soul's ability for versatility and the quest for equity.

All things considered, "Revealing Fortune Heists: Narratives of Wealth" has been a hypnotizing odyssey through the spellbinding universe of fortune heists, offering an all encompassing perspective on mankind's steadfast journey for riches and the significant effect it has had on social orders and people the same. These accounts have engaged and dazzled our minds as well as welcomed us to consider the persevering through charm of fortune, the moral inquiries it raises, and the complicated stories it winds around.

As we wrap this excursion up, we are left with a feeling of marvel and interest. The narratives of fortune heists advise us that set of experiences is loaded up with stories of daringness, tricky, and interest, as well as the persevering through journey for abundance and the fortunes that represent it. While a portion of these accounts have arrived at a resolution, many remain covered in secret, anticipating goal and conclusion.

"Narratives of Wealth" is an update that our reality is a gold mine of stories ready to be uncovered, each with its own exceptional mix of desire, experience, and interest. It is a demonstration of the persevering through human soul that proceeds to look for and commend the wealth that characterize our set of experiences and shape our future.

Eventually, the charm of fortune stays an immortal and general interest — an impression of the timeless quest for riches, influence, and the commitment of a more splendid, more extravagant future. As we pull back from the pages of this enthralling narrative, we are left with a recharged appreciation for the intricacies of the human soul and the persevering through force of the fortunes that have caught our aggregate creative mind all through the ages. The tale of fortune heists is nowhere near finished, as it proceeds to develop and charm us, similarly as it has for incalculable ages.

9.1 Summarizing the adventures and mysteries explored

In our excursion through the pages of "Divulging Fortune Heists: Narratives of Wealth," we have wandered into a charming domain loaded up with a rich embroidery of undertakings and secrets. These stories have taken us across time and landmasses, uncovering the dauntlessness and interest that have went with humankind's steady quest for riches and the fortunes that represent it.

Our odyssey initiated with an investigation of probably the earliest realized treasure heists. These old stories gave a verifiable setting to the unquenchable human longing to gather riches. The thieves who overcame the limits of old burial chambers and sanctuaries showed a mix of daringness, sly, and assurance that has been a sign of fortune heists all through the ages. These early capers established the groundwork for quite some time long adventure of fortune chasing and treasure-protecting.

As we traveled through time, we set forth on the high oceans close by privateers and pirates, those trying spirits who sought after wealth across the tremendous spread of the sea. The endeavors of eminent figures like Blackbeard, Chief Kidd, and Anne Bonny rejuvenated the violent universe of oceanic robbery, where fortune was a substantial award not too far off, and savagery was a dependable friend. These stories exemplified the crude daringness of the people who thought for even a moment to resist the law and society as they continued looking for riches.

Our investigation took us further into the captivating universe of terrific heists and bold escapades. The narratives of the burglary of the Mona Lisa by Vincenzo Peruggia and the adventures of the Pink Jaguar Posse exhibited the craft of sly and the excitement of high-stakes robbery. These accounts enlightened the unpredictable dance between crooks, policing, the universe of workmanship wrongdoing, where daringness was frequently coordinated with sharp tricks.

Continuing on, we dug into the universe of coordinated wrongdoing and the fabulous heists that caught the creative mind of general society. The adventures of figures like John Dillinger and the Incomparable Train Burglary group displayed the fastidious preparation and trying execution expected for such epic heists. These accounts stripped back the layers of aspiration and voracity, where the quest for abundance prompted rebellion and viciousness, making a permanent imprint on history.

The cutting edge period acquainted us with another type of fortune trackers and swashbucklers who dared to reveal wealth concealed underneath the sea's profundities. The tale of Mel Fisher and his mission to rescue the Atocha's fortunes exemplified the assurance and determination important to uncover fortunes tragically missing to the profundities of the ocean. These stories showed the combination of history, innovation, and aspiration in the determined quest for submerged abundance.

"Annals of Wealth" additionally drenched us in the cryptic universe of social bringing home, where the moral issues encompassing the arrival of taken ancient rarities to their nations of beginning became the overwhelming focus. The bringing home of the Elgin Marbles and the Benin Bronzes featured the intricate discussions encompassing the legitimate responsibility for legacy. These accounts uncovered the many-sided snare of legislative issues, morals, and history that encompass the universe of taken treasures, bringing up significant issues about the job of exhibition halls, states, and people in safeguarding and localizing social relics.

All through our excursion, one subject stayed steady: the persevering through appeal of fortune and the degree to which people and social orders will go to gain it. These accounts enlightened a significant human interest with riches, influence, and the fortunes that represent them. This interest, it turned out to be clear, was not limited by time or spot; it was a widespread yearning that had molded history itself.

However, underneath the outer layer of these dazzling stories lay the significant effect of fortune heists on people, networks, and countries. While certain heists prompted riches and brilliance for the culprits, they frequently abandoned a path of obliteration, fights in court, and moral binds. The outcomes of these heists were extensive, influencing the social and verifiable stories of the spots from which fortunes were taken, as well as the destinies of those included.

"Narratives of Wealth" likewise uncovered the continuous endeavors to secure and protect treasures. The foundation of galleries, secure vaults, and high level safety efforts addressed a critical reaction to the tireless danger of burglary. The account of the Isabella Stewart Gardner Historical center heist and the resulting endeavors to recuperate the taken craftsmanships highlighted the responsibility of establishments and policing to shield our common social legacy.

Our process acquainted us with the vigorous work of people, researchers, and activists who devoted their lives to the recuperation and safeguarding of taken treasures. Their steadfast assurance and devotion notwithstanding difficulty filled in as a demonstration of the unyielding human soul, the quest for equity, and the conservation of our social heritage.

All things being equal, "Uncovering Fortune Heists: Narratives of Wealth" has been an unprecedented odyssey through the universe of fortune heists, offering an all encompassing perspective on humankind's steady journey for riches and the significant effect it has had on social orders and people. These accounts have engaged and spellbound our minds as well as welcomed us to think about the persevering through charm of fortune, the moral inquiries it raises, and the complicated stories it winds around.

As we finish up this exceptional excursion, we are left with a feeling of miracle and interest. The narratives of fortune heists advise us that set of experiences is packed with stories of daringness, tricky, and interest, as well as the getting through mission for abundance and the fortunes that represent it. While a portion of these accounts have arrived at a resolution, many remain covered in secret, anticipating goal and conclusion.

"Narratives of Wealth" is an update that our reality is a mother lode of stories ready to be revealed, each with its own interesting mix of desire, experience, and interest. It is a demonstration of the persevering through human soul that proceeds to look for and praise the wealth that characterize our set of experiences and shape our future.

Eventually, the charm of fortune stays an immortal and all inclusive interest — an impression of the timeless quest for riches, influence, and the commitment of a more brilliant, more extravagant future. As we pull back from the pages of this enthralling narrative, we are left with a restored appreciation for the intricacies of the human soul and the getting through force of the fortunes that have caught our aggregate creative mind all through the ages. The account of fortune heists is nowhere near finished, as it proceeds to advance and spellbind us, similarly as it has for endless ages. These stories have shown that while the quest for wealth might prompt daring experiences and captivating secrets, eventually the human soul characterizes the genuine worth of these annals of wealth.

9.2 The enduring allure of treasure heists

The persevering through charm of fortune heists is a demonstration of the significant interest that mankind has held for abundance and the wealth that represent it all through the ages. These enrapturing stories, as investigated in "Disclosing Fortune Heists: Narratives of Wealth," have risen above time and topography, winding around an embroidery of daringness, tricky, and interest. This interest with treasure heists goes past the basic quest for material wealth; it addresses a well established longing for influence, extravagance, and the charm of the unexplored world.

Our excursion into the universe of fortune heists started with an investigation of probably the earliest occurrences of robbery and plundering. These antiquated stories uncovered that the mission for riches and the fortunes it involved have been important for the human experience for centuries. From thieves thinking for even a moment to wander into old burial places to flee with important relics to the people who ravaged respected sanctuaries, these accounts enlightened the boldness and assurance that have described treasure heists over the entire course of time. They set up for a considerable length of time long adventure of fortune chasing and treasure-monitoring.

As we traveled further into history, we set out on high-oceans experiences with privateers and marauders, those daring spirits who scoured the seas for wealth. The tales of figures like Blackbeard, Commander Kidd, and Anne Bonny rejuvenated the turbulent universe of oceanic robbery, where fortune was a definitive award not too far off, and brutality was a dependable friend. These stories highlighted the crude daringness of the people who resisted the law and cultural standards in their constant quest for riches.

Our investigation took us more profound into the domain of great heists and bold escapades. The nervy burglary of the Mona Lisa by Vincenzo Peruggia and the adventures of the Pink Jaguar Posse delineated the specialty of tricky and the excitement of high-stakes robbery. These accounts gave bits of knowledge into the perplexing dance between hoodlums, policing, the universe of workmanship wrongdoing, where daringness was frequently coordinated with shrewd tricks.

Forging ahead, we dug into the universe of coordinated wrongdoing, where brains like John Dillinger and the Incomparable Train Burglary posse arranged huge heists that made a permanent imprint on history. These accounts uncovered the careful preparation and trying execution expected for such excellent scale robberies. They stripped back the layers of desire and insatiability, uncovering that the quest for abundance could prompt rebellion and savagery, leaving enduring engravings on society and memory.

The cutting edge period introduced another variety of fortune trackers and travelers, trying to uncover wealth concealed underneath the sea's profundities. The story of Mel Fisher and his constant journey to rescue the Atocha's fortunes exemplified the assurance and diligence important to recuperate fortunes tragically missing to the ocean. These stories highlighted the combination of history, innovation, and desire in the tenacious quest for submerged riches.

"Narratives of Wealth" additionally submerged us in the cryptic universe of social bringing home, where the moral situations encompassing the arrival of taken antiquities to their nations of beginning became the overwhelming focus. The bringing home of the Elgin Marbles and the Benin Bronzes featured the complex discussions encompassing the legitimate responsibility for legacy. These accounts disentangled the mind boggling snare of legislative issues, morals, and history that covered the universe of taken treasures, bringing up significant issues about the job of galleries, states, and people in safeguarding and localizing social curios.

All through our excursion, one subject stayed steady: the getting through charm of fortune and the lengths to which people and social orders were able to go to procure it. These accounts shed light on a significant human interest with riches, influence, and the fortunes that represent them. This interest rose above overall setting; it was an all inclusive desire that had significantly molded history itself.

However, underneath the outer layer of these enamoring stories lay the significant effect of fortune heists on people, networks, and countries. While certain heists prompted wealth and magnificence for the culprits, they frequently abandoned a path of obliteration, fights in court, and moral issues. The results of these heists were expansive, influencing the social and authentic accounts of the spots from which fortunes were taken, as well as the destinies of those included.

"Annals of Wealth" additionally uncovered the continuous endeavors to safeguard and save treasures. The foundation of historical centers, secure vaults, and high level safety efforts addressed a critical reaction to the tireless danger of robbery. The account of the Isabella Stewart Gardner Exhibition hall heist and the resulting endeavors to recuperate the taken works of art highlighted the responsibility of establishments and policing to protect our common social legacy.

Our process acquainted us with the vigorous work of people, researchers, and activists who had devoted their lives to the recuperation and conservation of taken treasures. Their steadfast assurance and devotion even with misfortune filled in as a demonstration of the unyielding human soul, the quest for equity, and the protection of our social heritage.

All things being equal, "Disclosing Fortune Heists: Narratives of Wealth" has been an exceptional odyssey through the universe of fortune heists, offering an all encompassing perspective on humankind's persistent journey for riches and the significant effect it has had on social orders and people. These accounts have engaged and enamored our minds as well as welcomed us to ponder the getting through charm of fortune, the moral inquiries it raises, and the complicated stories it winds around.

As we finish up this noteworthy excursion, we are left with a feeling of marvel and interest. The accounts of fortune heists advise us that set of experiences is packed with stories of dauntlessness, sly, and interest, as well as the getting through mission for abundance and the fortunes that represent it. While a portion of these accounts have arrived at a resolution, many remain covered in secret, anticipating goal and conclusion.

"Narratives of Wealth" is an update that our reality is a mother lode of stories ready to be uncovered, each with its own one of a kind mix of desire, experience, and interest. It is a demonstration of the persevering through human soul that proceeds to look for and praise the wealth that characterize our set of experiences and shape our future.

The charm of fortune stays an immortal and general interest, mirroring the timeless quest for riches, influence, and the commitment of a more brilliant, more extravagant future. As we move back from the pages of this enamoring narrative, we are left with a recharged appreciation for the intricacies of the human soul and the getting through force of the fortunes that have caught our aggregate creative mind all through the ages. The account of fortune heists is nowhere near finished, as it proceeds to develop and enrapture us, similarly as it has for incalculable ages. These stories have shown that while the quest for wealth might prompt venturesome experiences and charming secrets, eventually the human soul characterizes the genuine worth of these annals of wealth.